FRENCH DESSERT COOKBOOK

600+ SWEET AND SAVORY FRENCH RECIPES TO SATISFY YOUR SWEET TOOTH

By
CARL J. PEREA

TABLE OF CONTENTS

CHAPTER:12 156

CANDIES AND MIGNARDISES 156

CHAPTER:13 170

SPECIAL OCCASION DESSERTS 170

CONCLUSION 199

INTRODUCTION

Welcome to the delectable world of French desserts! This French Dessert Cookbook is your passport to a culinary journey through the enchanting realm of exquisite pastries, velvety chocolates, and indulgent sweets that have captivated dessert enthusiasts for centuries.

French treats are known worldwide for being elegant, sophisticated, and full of complex flavors. From the delicate layers of a classic Mille-Feuille to the rich depths of a decadent Chocolate Mousse, French dessert-making celebrates art and taste. This cookbook will help you learn about the fascinating world of French desserts and give you the skills to make these delicious treats in your kitchen.

In this guide, you'll go on a tasty trip as you learn about the techniques, ingredients, and recipes that make French sweets special. From the delicate art of making pie dough to the exact science of melting chocolate, each recipe is carefully written so that both new and experienced bakers can get great results.

This recipe has something for every dessert lover, whether they want the silky smoothness of Crème Brûlée, the heavenly smell of a freshly baked Croissant, or the colorful beauty of a Macaron. With a collection of classic French desserts, new takes on old favorites, and lesser-known regional specialties, you will have a treasure trove of sweet treats.

In addition to the recipes, this book will teach you about the rich history and cultural importance of French treats. French treats are a big part of the country's culinary history, from the patisseries in Paris to the boulangeries in the country. By learning about the stories and customs behind these sweets, you'll better understand the skill and creativity that goes into making each one.

No matter how experienced you are in the kitchen or how new you are to baking, this French Dessert Cookbook will walk you through each recipe with clear instructions, helpful tips, and techniques to ensure success. With practice and care, you'll get the skills and confidence to master French desserts and make amazing dishes that will wow your family and friends.

So, put on your apron, heat the oven, and let the delicious smells of French treats fill your kitchen. This cookbook guides a world of delicious treats, from delicate cakes to splurge-worthy candies. With each recipe you try, you'll learn more about making French pastries and discover what makes these desserts so special.

Do you want to go on a sweet journey? Let this French Dessert Cookbook show you how to make sweet and happy memories that will last a lifetime.

CHAPTER:1

FOUNDATIONAL SKILLS: BASIC TECHNIQUES IN FRENCH PATISSERIE

Welcome to the first part of our guide to French pastries. In this part, "Foundational Skills: Basic Techniques in French Patisserie," we will look at the most important techniques that make up the art of making French pastries. This chapter will give you the basic skills to make delicious French sweets in your home. You will learn to make perfect pastry doughs, delicate creams, and sauces.

1.1 Pastry Doughs:

Pastry dough is the most important part of French pastry. This part will teach you the two most common types of pastry dough used in French baking: pate brisée and pate feuilletée. You will learn to make soft, buttery shortcrust pastry for pies and quiches. You will also learn how to make flaky, layered puff pastry for delicate desserts like croissants and mille-feuille, which is time-consuming.

1.2 Crème Pâtissière:

Crème patissière, also called "pastry cream," is a filling for French desserts like éclairs, cream puffs, and fruit pies made of a rich custard. This part will show you how to make a pastry cream that is smooth and soft and tastes like vanilla, chocolate, or coffee mixed into it. You will learn to soften eggs, make custard, and get the right filling consistency for your baked goods.

1.3 Chantilly Cream:

Chantilly cream, whipped cream, is a common ingredient in French pastries. You'll learn to whip cream to the right consistency in this part. You'll learn to avoid whipping it too much and get soft, billowy peaks. Chantilly cream is important to treats like pies, cakes, and mousses. It gives your products a bit of richness and grace.

1.4 Genoise Sponge Cake:

Genoise sponge cake is the base of many French sweets and desserts, such as the Fraisier and the Charlotte, both classics. This part will show you how to make an egg, sugar, flour, and butter sponge cake that is light and airy. You will learn to mix the ingredients correctly to make a soft, even-textured cake.

1.5 Meringue:

In French pastry, meringue is a flexible ingredient for light desserts like macarons, pavlovas, and pies. This part will discuss the two main kinds of meringue: French and Italian. You will learn how to whisk egg whites until they form stiff peaks, add sugar, and get the right thickness for your desserts made with meringue.

1.6 Caramelization:

Caramelization is a key step in French pastry making that gives sweets more depth and flavor. This part will show you how to caramelize sugar to make caramel sauces, artistic caramel cages, or crunchy caramelized treats. You will learn the different steps of caramelization and how to control the process to get the taste and color you want.

1.7 Decorative Techniques:

In French pastry, how things look is very important. In this part, you'll learn different ways to decorate your desserts to make them look like works of art. You will learn how to use a piping bag and different tips to make detailed designs with piping, as well as how to glaze, dust with powdered sugar, and decorate with fruits or chocolate. With these skills, you'll be able to make things as beautiful to look at as they are to eat.

By getting good at the basic skills and methods in this chapter, you will feel ready to dive into French pastry. Whether you want to make tiny pies, as light as air cookies, or rich, layered cakes, these skills will help you get there. Remember that practice is the best way to learn, so roll up your sleeves, get ready to measure, whisk, and fold, and let your cooking imagination soar as you enter the beautiful world of French pastry-making.

CHAPTER:2
SIGNATURE PASTRIES: ICONIC FRENCH DESSERTS

Welcome to the second part of our guide to French pastries. In this chapter, "Signature Pastries: Iconic French Desserts," we'll learn about the most famous and popular French sweets. From the airy layers of a croissant to the delicate beauty of a macaron, this chapter will introduce you to the famous sweets that have won the hearts and stomachs of pastry lovers worldwide.

2.1 Croissant:

The croissant's buttery, fluffy layers and delicate circular form make it a sign of French baking. This part will show you how to make this well-known treat from scratch. You will learn how to make famous croissants that are both crispy and soft. You will learn to butter the dough and get the perfect golden-brown crust.

2.2 Macaron:

The macaron is a tiny, colorful dessert made with almond flour that has become a true French specialty. In this part, we'll explain how to make these cute sandwich cookies. You will learn the careful folding technique that gives macarons their smooth, shiny surface. You will also try out different fillings and flavor combinations that will make you feel like you're in a bakery in Paris.

2.3 Tarte Tatin:

Tarte Tatin is a caramelized upside-down apple tart that has become a timeless classic in French cuisine. In this section, you will learn the technique of caramelizing apples to create a rich and sticky caramel sauce. You will also master assembling and baking the tart to achieve a golden crust and perfectly tender apples. Serve it warm with a dollop of whipped cream or a scoop of vanilla ice cream for a truly indulgent dessert.

2.4 Éclair:

The éclair is a long, cream-filled pastry topped with a glossy chocolate glaze. This section will guide you through creating choux pastry—the light and airy dough that forms the base of éclairs. You will learn to pipe the dough into the classic elongated shape and fill it with luscious pastry cream. Finally, you will master creating a glossy chocolate glaze to top off your éclairs with elegance.

2.5 Mille-Feuille:

Mille-feuille, meaning "thousand layers," is a delicate pastry of crisp puff layers sandwiched with luscious pastry cream. This section will teach you how to make puff pastry from scratch or use store-bought dough for convenience. You will learn the technique of creating uniform layers of pastry and filling them with silky pastry cream. The finishing touch involves a dusting of powdered sugar and a decorative touch, resulting in a visually stunning dessert.

2.6 Profiteroles:

Profiteroles are small, cream-filled choux pastries drizzled with a rich chocolate sauce. In this section, you will learn the techniques for creating light and puffy choux pastry and piping them into small rounds. You will also explore variations of fillings, such as whipped cream or ice cream, and how to assemble and garnish these delectable treats.

2.7 Opera Cake:

The Opera cake is a rich, layered with almond sponge cake, coffee icing, and chocolate frosting. This section will show you how to combine each part to make a beautiful cake. You will learn how to make sponge cake that is moist and tasty, buttercream that is smooth, and ganache that is shiny. The result is a fancy treat that will definitely please.

As you try these famous French sweets, it's important to pay close attention to the details and be exact. Take your time to learn each skill, enjoy the process, and then enjoy the results of your hard work. Whether you're serving these pastries for a special event or just giving yourself a little treat, they'll take you back to the lovely patisseries of France, where the art of making pastries is truly praised.

CHAPTER:3

DECADENT CHOCOLATES AND CONFECTIONS: MASTERING FRENCH SWEETS

In this book, titled "Decadent Chocolates and Confections: Mastering French Sweets," we will dive into the world of indulgent chocolates, delicate candies, and exquisite confections that are synonymous with the art of French pastry-making. Get ready to tantalize your taste buds and discover the secrets behind creating irresistible sweet treats.

3.1 Truffles:

Truffles are luxurious, bite-sized confections with rich chocolate ganache coated in cocoa powder or other delectable coatings. This section will teach you how to create a silky smooth ganache infused with flavors like vanilla, espresso, or liqueurs. You will also explore various methods of shaping and coating the truffles, allowing you to unleash your creativity and customize these irresistible treats.

3.2 Chocolate Mousse:

Chocolate mousse is a velvety, airy dessert that combines chocolate's richness with whipped cream's lightness. This section will guide you through creating a smooth and luscious chocolate mousse, using techniques like folding whipped cream into melted chocolate to achieve the perfect texture. You will also be able to experiment with flavor variations, such as dark chocolate, white chocolate, or even infused with spices or liqueurs.

3.3 Caramel:

Caramel is a staple in French confections, adding a rich and sweet flavor to various treats. In this section, you will learn the art of caramelization, from creating a golden caramel sauce to crafting delicate caramel decorations. You will also explore different types of caramel, including soft and chewy caramel candies and crunchy caramel shards that can elevate the presentation of your desserts.

3.4 Ganache:

Ganache is a versatile and velvety mixture of chocolate and cream that is a foundation for many French sweets. This section will teach you the techniques to create a perfectly balanced ganache, whether for filling pastries, glazing cakes, or making truffles. You will explore the interplay of different chocolate percentages and experiment with flavorings like fruits, spices, or liqueurs to create unique and decadent ganache creations.

3.5 Pralines:

Pralines are a beloved French confection made with caramelized nuts, often coated in chocolate. In this section, you will learn how to prepare crunchy and caramelized nuts, such as almonds or hazelnuts, and create a delectable praline paste for various desserts. You will also discover techniques for molding and coating pralines in chocolate, resulting in delightful treats that combine sweetness and nutty flavors.

3.6 Nougat:

Nougat is a chewy and nut-filled confection that dates back centuries in French confectionery tradition. This section will guide you through creating traditional nougat, incorporating ingredients like almonds, pistachios, or dried fruits into a sticky and sweet base. You will learn the technique of cooking the sugar syrup to the precise temperature and the art of achieving the perfect balance of chewiness and tenderness in your nougat.

3.7 Pâte de Fruits:

Pate de fruits, also known as fruit jellies, are sweets made with concentrated fruit purees that are bright and tasty. In this part, you will learn how to make these delicious treats from scratch by mixing fruit juice, sugar, and pectin. You will learn to set the fruit blend to be soft and chewy. This will give you bite-sized candies that taste like real fruit.

Indulging in French chocolates and sweets gives you a chance to see the beauty and skill that goes into making these delicious treats. From rich truffles to creamy mousses, crunchy pralines to chewy nougat, these French sweets will wake up your feelings and make you happy with every bite.

As you go through this chapter, enjoy the steps you must take to make these delicious treats. Try different tastes, textures, and decorations to make your projects your own. Remember that working with chocolate and other delicate sweets requires accuracy and careful attention to detail, so take your time and enjoy the art of fine crafting.

Whether planning a special event or just wanting a moment of sweet bliss, the skills and techniques you learn in this chapter will help you master the art of French candies and sweets. So, get your fixings together, let your imagination run wild, and let the magic of French sweets take you to a world of unmatched pleasure.

CHAPTER:4
HOMEY CAKES

MIEL ET LAVANDE CAKE (HONEY AND LAVENDER CAKE):

INGREDIENTS:

- 1 3/4 cups all-purpose flour
- 2 teaspoons baking powder
- 1/4 teaspoon salt
- 1/2 cup unsalted butter, softened
- 1/2 cup granulated sugar
- 2 tablespoons honey
- 2 large eggs
- 1 teaspoon vanilla extract
- 1 tablespoon dried culinary lavender
- 1/2 cup milk
- Lavender sprigs (for garnish)
  For the Honey Glaze:
- 1/4 cup honey
- 1 tablespoon lemon juice

INSTRUCTIONS:

1. Set your oven to 350°F (175°C) and turn it on. Coat a round cake pan with butter and flour.
2. Mix the flour, baking powder, and salt in a bowl with a whisk.
3. In a different big bowl, beat the butter, sugar, and honey until they are light and fluffy.
4. Add the eggs one by one and mix well after each one. Add the vanilla extract and mix well.
5. Alternate adding the dry ingredients and the milk to the butter mixture, starting and ending with the dry ingredients. Mix until just mixed.
6. Gently add the dried lavender.

7. Pour the batter into the cake pan that has already been greased, and use a spatula to smooth the top.
8. Bake in an oven that has been warm for 25 to 30 minutes or until a toothpick stuck in the middle comes out clean.
9. Make the honey glaze while the cake is still warm by heating the honey and lemon juice in a small pot until they mix. Take off the heat.
10. Make small holes in the top of the cake with a toothpick. Drizzle the honey sauce over the holes in the cake and let it soak in.
11. Let the cake cool down in the pan before taking it out. Add sprigs of lavender to the top.
12. Cut the Miel et Lavande Cake into pieces and serve it.

GÂTEAU DE MIEL ET D'AMANDES (HONEY ALMOND CAKE):

INGREDIENTS:

- 1 1/2 cups all-purpose flour
- 1/2 cup almond flour
- 2 teaspoons baking powder
- 1/4 teaspoon salt
- 1/2 cup unsalted butter, softened
- 1/2 cup granulated sugar
- 1/2 cup honey
- 3 large eggs
- 1 teaspoon almond extract
- 1/2 cup milk
- 1/4 cup sliced almonds (for topping)
  For the Honey Glaze:
- 1/4 cup honey
- 1 tablespoon lemon juice

INSTRUCTIONS:

1. Set your oven to 350°F (175°C) and turn it on. Coat a round cake pan with butter and flour.

2. Mix the all-purpose flour, almond flour, baking powder, and salt in a bowl with a whisk.
3. In a different big bowl, beat the butter, sugar, and honey until they are light and fluffy.
4. Add the eggs one by one and mix well after each one. Add the almond flavor and mix well.
5. Alternate adding the dry ingredients and the milk to the butter mixture, starting and ending with the dry ingredients. Mix until just mixed.
6. Pour the batter into the cake pan that has already been greased, and use a spatula to smooth the top.
7. Spread the sliced nuts out over the top of the batter in an even layer.
8. Bake in an oven that has been warm for 25 to 30 minutes or until a toothpick stuck in the middle comes out clean.
9. Make the honey glaze while the cake is still warm by heating the honey and lemon juice in a small pot until they mix. Take off the heat.
10. Make small holes in the top of the cake with a toothpick. Drizzle the honey sauce over the holes in the cake and let it soak in.
11. Let the cake cool down in the pan before taking it out.
12. Slice and serve the Gateau de Miel et d'Amandes.

HONEY MADELEINE CAKE:

INGREDIENTS:
- 1/2 cup unsalted butter, melted and cooled
- 2/3 cup granulated sugar
- 2 tablespoons honey
- 2 large eggs
- 1 teaspoon vanilla extract
- 1 cup all-purpose flour
- 1/2 teaspoon baking powder
- Pinch of salt
- Powdered sugar (for dusting)

INSTRUCTIONS:
1. Set your oven to 375°F (190°C) to get it ready. Coat madeleine shapes or a madeleine pan with butter and flour.
2. Whisk the melted butter, sugar, honey, eggs, and vanilla extract together until everything is well-mixed.
3. Mix the all-purpose flour, baking powder, and salt separately.
4. Slowly add the dry ingredients to the wet ingredients and stir until they are mixed.
5. Fill the madeleine shapes about 3/4 of the way with the batter.
6. Bake the madeleines in an oven that has already been warm for 10 to 12 minutes, or until the edges are golden and bounce back when lightly pressed.
7. Take the madeleines out of the oven and let them cool for a few minutes in the pan before moving them to a wire rack to cool fully.
8. Before serving, the Honey Madeleine Cake is dusted with powdered sugar.

GÂTEAU AU YAOURT ET AUX MYRTILLES (BLUEBERRY YOGURT CAKE):

INGREDIENTS:

- 1 1/2 cups all-purpose flour
- 2 teaspoons baking powder
- 1/4 teaspoon salt
- 1 cup plain yogurt
- 1 cup granulated sugar
- 3 large eggs
- 1/2 cup vegetable oil
- 1 teaspoon vanilla extract
- 1 1/2 cups fresh blueberries

INSTRUCTIONS:

1. Set your oven to 350°F (175°C) and turn it on. Coat a round cake pan with butter and flour.
2. Mix the flour, baking powder, and salt in a bowl with a whisk.
3. Whisk together the yogurt, sugar, eggs, vegetable oil, and vanilla extract in a separate big bowl until they are well mixed.
4. Mix the dry ingredients with the wet ingredients in a slow, steady stream until they are mixed.
5. Gently add the fresh blueberries.
6. Pour the batter into the cake pan that has already been greased, and use a spatula to smooth the top.
7. Bake in an oven that has been warm for 30–35 minutes or until a toothpick stuck in the middle comes out clean.
8. After 10 minutes, take the cake from the pan and put it on a wire rack to cool fully.
9. Slice and serve the Gateau au Yaourt et aux Myrtilles.

GÂTEAU BRETON (BRITTANY BUTTER CAKE):

INGREDIENTS:
- 1 1/2 cups all-purpose flour
- 1 1/4 cups unsalted butter, softened
- 1 cup granulated sugar
- 4 large egg yolks
- 1 teaspoon vanilla extract
- Pinch of salt

INSTRUCTIONS:
1. Set your oven to 350°F (175°C) and turn it on. Coat a round cake pan with butter and flour.
2. Mix the butter and sugar in a bowl until light and fluffy.
3. Add the egg yolks one at a time, making sure to beat well after each. Add the vanilla extract and mix well.
4. Mix the flour and salt into the butter mixture until it is mixed.
5. Press the dough evenly into the cake pan, and use a spatula to smooth the top.
6. Make a zigzag design on the top of the cake with a fork.
7. Bake for 30–35 minutes in an oven that has already been warm or until the edges are golden brown.
8. After 10 minutes, take the cake from the pan and put it on a wire rack to cool fully.
9. Slice the Gateau Breton and serve it.

GÂTEAU DE SAVOIE (SAVOIE SPONGE CAKE):

INGREDIENTS:
- 6 large eggs, separated
- 1 cup granulated sugar
- 1 teaspoon vanilla extract
- 1 cup all-purpose flour
- 1/4 teaspoon salt
- Powdered sugar (for dusting)

INSTRUCTIONS:
1. Set your oven to 350°F (175°C) and turn it on. Coat a round cake pan with butter and flour.
2. Beat the egg whites, sugar, and vanilla extract until the mixture is thick and pale yellow.
3. Mix the flour and salt in a different bowl with a whisk.
4. Gradually add the flour mixture to the egg yolk mixture and stir until just mixed.
5. Beat the egg whites in another bowl until stiff peaks form.
6. Fold the beaten egg whites in gently until they are well mixed in.
7. Pour the batter into the cake pan that has already been greased, and use a spatula to smooth the top.
8. Bake in an oven that has been warm for 30–35 minutes or until a toothpick stuck in the middle comes out clean.
9. After 10 minutes, take the cake from the pan and put it on a wire rack to cool fully.
10. Before you serve the Gateau de Savoie, dust it with powdered sugar.

MOELLEUX AU CHOCOLAT (CHOCOLATE FONDANT CAKE):

INGREDIENTS:

- 8 ounces dark chocolate, chopped
- 1/2 cup unsalted butter
- 1/2 cup granulated sugar
- 4 large eggs
- 1/4 cup all-purpose flour
- Pinch of salt
- Powdered sugar (for dusting)

INSTRUCTIONS:

1. Set your oven to 350°F (175°C) and turn it on. Coat a round cake pan with butter and flour.
2. Mix dark chocolate and butter in a bowl that can handle the heat. You can do this in the microwave or over a double boiler.
3. Mix the granulated sugar, eggs, flour, and salt in a different bowl until they are well mixed.
4. Gradually add the chocolate mixture that has been melted to the egg mixture and stir until smooth.
5. Pour the batter into the cake pan that has already been greased, and use a spatula to smooth the top.
6. Bake in an oven that has already been warm for 20 to 25 minutes, or until the edges are set, and the middle is still slightly soft.
7. Let the cake cool for 10 minutes in the pan, then move it to a plate to serve.
8. Before you serve the Moelleux au Chocolat, dust it with powdered sugar.

GÂTEAU AUX NOISETTES (HAZELNUT CAKE):

INGREDIENTS:
- 1 cup hazelnuts, toasted and finely ground
- 1 cup all-purpose flour
- 1 teaspoon baking powder
- 1/4 teaspoon salt
- 1/2 cup unsalted butter, softened
- 1 cup granulated sugar
- 4 large eggs
- 1 teaspoon vanilla extract
- Powdered sugar (for dusting)

INSTRUCTIONS:
1. Set your oven to 350°F (175°C) and turn it on. Coat a round cake pan with butter and flour.
2. Mix the ground hazelnuts, flour, baking powder, and salt in a bowl.
3. Mix the butter and sugar together in a different big bowl until they are light and fluffy.
4. Add the eggs one by one and mix well after each one. Add the vanilla extract and mix well.
5. Mix the dry ingredients into the butter mixture little by little until they are just mixed in.
6. Pour the batter into the cake pan that has already been greased, and use a spatula to smooth the top.
7. Bake in an oven that has been warm for 30–35 minutes or until a toothpick stuck in the middle comes out clean.
8. After 10 minutes, take the cake from the pan and put it on a wire rack to cool fully.
9. Before you serve the Gateau aux Noisettes, dust it with powdered sugar.

GÂTEAU AUX AMANDES ET AU MIEL (ALMOND HONEY CAKE):

INGREDIENTS:
- 1 1/2 cups almond flour
- 1/2 cup all-purpose flour
- 1/2 teaspoon baking powder
- 1/4 teaspoon salt
- 1/2 cup unsalted butter, softened
- 3/4 cup granulated sugar
- 3 large eggs
- 1/4 cup honey
- 1/4 cup milk
- 1 teaspoon almond extract
- Sliced almonds (for topping)
- Powdered sugar (for dusting)

INSTRUCTIONS:
1. Set your oven to 350°F (175°C) and turn it on. Coat a round cake pan with butter and flour.
2. Mix the almond flour, all-purpose flour, baking powder, and salt in a bowl with a whisk.
3. Mix the butter and sugar together in a different big bowl until they are light and fluffy.
4. Add the eggs one by one and mix well after each one. Mix in the almond extract, honey, and milk.
5. Mix the dry ingredients into the butter mixture little by little until they are just mixed in.
6. Pour the batter into the cake pan that has already been greased, and use a spatula to smooth the top.
7. Spread the sliced nuts out over the top of the batter in an even layer.
8. Bake in an oven that has been warm for 30–35 minutes or until a toothpick stuck in the middle comes out clean.
9. After 10 minutes, take the cake from the pan and put it on a wire rack to cool fully.

10. Before you serve the Gateau aux Amandes et au Miel, dust it with powdered sugar.

QUATRE-QUARTS AUX POMMES (FRENCH POUND CAKE WITH APPLES):

INGREDIENTS:

- 1 1/2 cups all-purpose flour
- 1 teaspoon baking powder
- 1/4 teaspoon salt
- 1 cup unsalted butter, softened
- 1 cup granulated sugar
- 4 large eggs
- 1 teaspoon vanilla extract
- 2 apples, peeled, cored, and sliced
- Powdered sugar (for dusting)

INSTRUCTIONS:

1. Set your oven to 350°F (175°C) and turn it on. Coat a loaf pan with oil and flour.
2. Mix the flour, baking powder, and salt in a bowl with a whisk.
3. Mix the butter and sugar together in a different big bowl until they are light and fluffy.
4. Add the eggs one by one and mix well after each one. Add the vanilla extract and mix well.
5. Mix the dry ingredients into the butter mixture little by little until they are just mixed in.
6. Pour half the batter into the loaf pan that has been made. Place the apple slices on top, then pour the rest of the batter over them.
7. Bake in an oven that has been warm for 50 to 60 minutes or until a toothpick stuck in the middle comes out clean.
8. After 10 minutes, take the cake from the pan and put it on a wire rack to cool fully.
9. Before you serve the Quatre-Quarts aux Pommes, dust it with powdered sugar.

GÂTEAU AU FROMAGE BLANC ET AUX FRAISES (STRAWBERRY CHEESECAKE):

INGREDIENTS:
- 1 1/2 cups graham cracker crumbs
- 1/4 cup unsalted butter, melted
- 16 ounces cream cheese, softened
- 1 cup granulated sugar
- 1 teaspoon vanilla extract
- 4 large eggs
- 1 cup sour cream
- 2 cups fresh strawberries, sliced
- Strawberry sauce (for topping)

INSTRUCTIONS:
1. Set your oven to 325°F (160°C) and turn it on. Grease and line with parchment paper a springform pan.
2. Mix the graham cracker crumbs and melted butter together in a bowl. Press the batter into the bottom of the pan set up to make the crust.
3. In a different big bowl, beat the cream cheese, sugar, and vanilla extract together until smooth.
4. Add the eggs one by one and mix well after each one. Add the sour cream and mix.
5. Pour the cream cheese mixture on top of the bread in the pan.
6. Bake in a warmed oven for 50 to 60 minutes until the middle is set and the top is lightly golden.
7. After 10 minutes, remove the cheesecake from the pan and put it on a wire rack to cool fully.
8. Refrigerate the cheesecake for at least 4 hours or overnight.
9. Before serving, put strawberry slices on top of the Gateau au Fromage Blanc et aux Fraises and drizzle it with strawberry sauce.

GÂTEAU BASQUE À LA CRÈME PÂTISSIÈRE (BASQUE CAKE WITH PASTRY CREAM):

INGREDIENTS:

For the Pastry Cream:
- 2 cups whole milk
- 4 egg yolks
- 1/2 cup granulated sugar
- 1/4 cup cornstarch
- 1 teaspoon vanilla extract

For the Basque Cake:
- 2 cups all-purpose flour
- 1 teaspoon baking powder
- 1/4 teaspoon salt
- 3/4 cup unsalted butter, softened
- 1 cup granulated sugar
- 2 large eggs
- 1 teaspoon vanilla extract
- Pastry cream (prepared from the above ingredients)
- Egg wash (1 egg yolk mixed with 1 tablespoon milk)
- Sliced almonds (for topping)

INSTRUCTIONS:

1. Heat the milk in a pot over medium heat for the pastry cream until it starts to steam but doesn't boil.
2. Whisk the egg whites, sugar, and cornstarch until well mixed.
3. Pour the hot milk into the egg mixture slowly while mixing.
4. Return the liquid to the pot and cook it over medium heat, mixing it constantly until it thickens.
5. Take it off the heat and add the vanilla extract. Put the pastry cream in a bowl and let it cool down.
6. To make a Basque Cake:
7. Set your oven to 350°F (175°C) and turn it on. Coat a round cake pan with butter and flour.
8. Mix the flour, baking powder, and salt in a bowl with a whisk.

9. Mix the butter and sugar together in a different big bowl until they are light and fluffy.
10. Add the eggs one by one and mix well after each one. Add the vanilla extract and mix well.
11. Mix the dry ingredients into the butter mixture little by little until they are just mixed in.
12. Cut the dough in two. Press one-half of the dough into the bottom of the cake pan.
13. Spread the pastry cream over the dough in the pan to be even.
14. Roll out the rest of the dough on a floured surface and place it on top of the pastry cream. Seal the sides with the dough on the bottom layer.
15. Spread an egg wash over the top of the cake and sprinkle it with sliced almonds.
16. Bake for 40–45 minutes in an oven that has already been warm or until the top is golden brown.
17. After 10 minutes, take the cake from the pan and put it on a wire rack to cool fully.

GÂTEAU INVISIBLE AUX POMMES (INVISIBLE APPLE CAKE):

INGREDIENTS:
- 4 medium apples, peeled and thinly sliced
- 2 tablespoons lemon juice
- 3/4 cup all-purpose flour
- 1/4 cup granulated sugar
- 1 teaspoon baking powder
- Pinch of salt
- 3 large eggs
- 1/2 cup milk
- 2 tablespoons unsalted butter, melted
- Powdered sugar (for dusting)

INSTRUCTIONS:

1. Set your oven to 350°F (175°C) and turn it on. Coat a round cake pan with butter and flour.
2. Toss the apple pieces in a bowl with lemon juice to keep them from going brown.
3. Whisk the flour, sugar, baking powder, and salt separately.
4. Mix the eggs, milk, and melted butter in another bowl with a whisk.
5. Whisk the dry ingredients into the egg mixture in small amounts until the mixture is smooth.
6. Fold the apple slices in gently until the batter covers them well.
7. Spread the batter out evenly in the ready cake pan.
8. Bake in an oven that has already been warm for 35 to 40 minutes or until a toothpick stuck in the middle comes out clean.
9. After 10 minutes, take the cake from the pan and put it on a wire rack to cool fully.
10. Before you serve the Gateau Invisible aux Pommes, dust it with powdered sugar.

MOELLEUX AUX POIRES ET AU CHOCOLAT (PEAR CHOCOLATE SOFT CAKE):

INGREDIENTS:
- 2 ripe pears, peeled, cored, and sliced
- 1 tablespoon lemon juice
- 4 ounces dark chocolate, chopped
- 1/2 cup unsalted butter
- 1/2 cup granulated sugar
- 3 large eggs
- 1/2 cup all-purpose flour
- Pinch of salt
- Powdered sugar (for dusting)

INSTRUCTIONS:

1. Set your oven to 350°F (175°C) and turn it on. Coat a round cake pan with butter and flour.
2. Toss the pear slices in a bowl with lemon juice
3. to keep them from getting brown.
4. Mix dark chocolate and butter in a bowl that can handle the heat. You can do this in the microwave or over a double boiler.
5. Mix the sugar and eggs in a different bowl until they are well mixed.
6. Whisk the flour and salt into the egg mixture in small amounts until the mixture is smooth.
7. Pour the melting chocolate into the eggs and stir until everything is well-mixed.
8. Fold the pear slices into the batter until they are spread out evenly.
9. Spread the batter out evenly in the ready cake pan.
10. Bake in an oven that has already been warm for 30–35 minutes, or until the top is set and the middle is still soft.
11. After 10 minutes, take the cake from the pan and put it on a wire rack to cool fully.
12. Before you serve the Moelleux aux Poires et au Chocolat, dust it with powdered sugar.

PAIN D'ÉPICES (SPICED HONEY CAKE):

INGREDIENTS:
- 2 1/2 cups all-purpose flour
- 2 teaspoons baking powder
- 1 teaspoon baking soda
- 1 teaspoon ground cinnamon
- 1/2 teaspoon ground ginger
- 1/4 teaspoon ground cloves
- 1/4 teaspoon ground nutmeg
- 1/4 teaspoon ground allspice
- 1/4 teaspoon salt
- 1/2 cup unsalted butter, melted

- 1/2 cup granulated sugar
- 1/2 cup honey
- 1 cup milk
- 1/4 cup molasses

INSTRUCTIONS:

1. Set your oven's temperature to 350°F (175°C). Flour and grease a loaf pan.
2. Mix the flour, baking powder, baking soda, spices, and salt in a bowl with a whisk.
3. Whisk the melted butter, sugar, honey, milk, and molasses in a separate big bowl until they are well mixed.
4. Gradually add the dry ingredients to the wet ingredients, stirring until mixed.
5. Pour the batter into the loaf pan that has been prepared, and use a spoon to smooth the top.
6. Bake in an oven that has already been warm for 50 to 60 minutes or until a toothpick in the middle comes out clean.
7. Let the cake cool for 10 minutes in the pan, and then move it to a wire rack to cool fully.
8. Slice the Pain d'Épices and serve it.

GÂTEAU DE RIZ (RICE PUDDING CAKE):

INGREDIENTS:

- 1 cup rice
- 4 cups milk
- 1/2 cup granulated sugar
- 1 teaspoon vanilla extract
- 4 eggs, separated
- Pinch of salt
- Butter (for greasing the pan)
- Cinnamon and powdered sugar (for dusting)

INSTRUCTIONS:

1. Set your oven to 350°F (175°C) and turn it on. Use butter to grease a round cake pan.

2. Follow the directions on the box to cook the rice in a pot with water. Drain and put away.
3. In a different pot, heat the milk on medium heat until it starts to steam but doesn't boil.
4. Whisk the sugar, vanilla extract, egg whites, and a pinch of salt together in a bowl.
5. Pour the hot milk into the egg mixture slowly while mixing.
6. Put the mixture back in the pot and cook it over low heat, turning it until it thickens.
7. Take it off the heat and add the cooked rice.
8. Beat the egg whites in a different bowl until stiff peaks form.
9. Fold the egg whites gently into the rice mixture until everything is well mixed.
10. Pour the batter into the cake pan that has already been greased, and use a spoon to smooth the top.
11. Bake for 30–35 minutes in an oven that has already been warm or until the top is golden brown.
12. Let the cake cool for 10 minutes in the pan, then move it to a plate to serve.
13. Before serving, sprinkle the Gateau de Riz with cinnamon and powdered sugar.

GÂTEAU DE CRÊPES (LAYERED CREPE CAKE):

INGREDIENTS:

For the Crêpes:
- 2 cups all-purpose flour
- 4 eggs
- 2 cups milk
- 1/4 cup granulated sugar
- 1 teaspoon vanilla extract
- Pinch of salt
- Butter (for greasing the pan)

For the Filling:
- Whipped cream, Nutella, fruit preserves, or any desired filling

INSTRUCTIONS:

1. Mix the flour, eggs, milk, sugar, vanilla extract, and salt in a bowl with a whisk until smooth.
2. Heat a skillet or crêpe pan that doesn't stick over medium heat. Use a little butter to grease the pan.
3. Pour a ladleful of batter into the pan and swirl it around to make a thin, even crêpe.
4. Cook the crêpe for about a minute or until the sides lift. Turn the crêpe over and cook it for another 30 seconds.
5. Put the cooked crêpe on a plate and do the same with the rest of the batter. As the crêpes cook, stack them on each other, saving a few for the top layer.
6. Spread a thin layer of whipped cream, Nutella, or fruit preserves on each crêpe once they are all cooked and cooled.
7. Stack the crêpes filled on top of each other to make a cake with layers. Put the crêpes that you saved on top.
8. Put the Gateau de Crêpes in the fridge for at least 2 hours to set the layers.
9. Slice the Gateau de Crêpes and serve it.

GÂTEAU AU CARAMEL ET BEURRE SALÉ (SALTED BUTTER CARAMEL CAKE):

INGREDIENTS:

For the Cake:
- 1 1/2 cups all-purpose flour
- 2 teaspoons baking powder
- 1/4 teaspoon salt
- 1/2 cup unsalted butter, softened
- 1 cup granulated sugar
- 2 large eggs
- 1 teaspoon vanilla extract
- 1/2 cup milk

For the Salted Butter Caramel:
- 1 cup granulated sugar
- 1/2 cup unsalted butter
- 1/2 cup heavy cream
- 1/4 teaspoon sea salt

INSTRUCTIONS:

1. P heat your oven to 350°F (175°C). Coat a round cake pan with butter and flour.
2. Mix the flour, baking powder, and salt in a bowl with a whisk.
3. Mix the butter and sugar together in a different big bowl until they are light and fluffy.
4. Add the eggs one by one and mix well after each one. Add the vanilla extract and mix well.
5. Alternate adding the dry ingredients and the milk to the butter mixture, starting and ending with the dry ingredients.
6. Pour the batter into the cake pan that has already been greased, and use a spatula to smooth the top.
7. Bake in an oven that has been warm for 25 to 30 minutes or until a toothpick stuck in the middle comes out clean.
8. After 10 minutes, take the cake from the pan and put it on a wire rack to cool fully.
9. Heat the granulated sugar in a pot over medium heat to make salted butter caramel until it melts and turns golden brown.

10. Add the butter and stir until it has melted and everything is mixed well.
11. Pour the heavy cream in slowly while stirring all the time. Be careful because the blend might start to bubble.
12. Mix in the sea salt until it is well mixed in.
13. Let the caramel cool before dumping it over the cool cake and running it down the sides.
14. Slice and serve the Gateau au Caramel et Beurre Salé.

GÂTEAU NANTAIS (ALMOND AND RUM CAKE FROM NANTES):

INGREDIENTS:
For the Cake:
- 1 cup almond flour
- 1/2 cup all-purpose flour
- 1 cup granulated sugar
- 1/2 cup unsalted butter, softened
- 4 large eggs
- 2 tablespoons dark rum
- 1/4 teaspoon almond extract

For the Rum Syrup:
- 1/2 cup granulated sugar
- 1/4 cup water
- 2 tablespoons dark rum

INSTRUCTIONS:
1. Set your oven to 350°F (175°C) and turn it on. Coat a round cake pan with butter and flour.
2. Mix the almond flour, all-purpose flour, and powdered sugar in a bowl with a whisk.
3. In a separate big bowl, cream the softened butter, eggs, rum, and almond flavor until well mixed.
4. Gradually add the dry ingredients to the butter mixture and stir until mixed.

5. Pour the batter into the cake pan that has already been greased, and use a spatula to smooth the top.
6. Bake in an oven that has already been warm for 35 to 40 minutes or until a toothpick stuck in the middle comes out clean.
7. While the cake is baking, make the rum syrup by putting the granulated sugar and water in a pot. Heat over medium heat until the sugar is dissolved.
8. Take the syrup off the heat and add the dark rum while stirring.
9. When the cake is done, take it out of the oven and let it cool for 10 minutes in the pan.
10. Use a stick or skewer to poke holes all over the top of the cake.
11. Pour the rum sauce over the warm cake in an even layer and let it soak in.
12. Let the cake cool in the pan before serving it to a plate.
13. Slice the Gateau Nantais and serve it.

GÂTEAU AUX CAROTTES (FRENCH CARROT CAKE):

INGREDIENTS:

For the Cake:
- 2 cups all-purpose flour
- 1 1/2 teaspoons baking powder
- 1/2 teaspoon baking soda
- 1/2 teaspoon salt
- 1 teaspoon ground cinnamon
- 1/2 teaspoon ground nutmeg
- 1/2 cup unsalted butter, softened
- 1 cup granulated sugar
- 2 large eggs
- 1 teaspoon vanilla extract
- 2 cups grated carrots

- 1/2 cup chopped walnuts or pecans (optional)
  For the Cream Cheese Frosting:
- 8 ounces cream cheese, softened
- 1/2 cup unsalted butter, softened
- 2 cups powdered sugar
- 1 teaspoon vanilla extract

INSTRUCTIONS:

1. Set your oven to 350°F (175°C) and turn it on. Coat a round cake pan with butter and flour.
2. Mix the flour, baking powder, baking soda, salt, cinnamon, and nutmeg with a whisk.
3. In a separate big bowl, beat the melted butter and powdered sugar until they are light and fluffy.
4. Add the eggs one by one and mix well after each one. Add the vanilla extract and mix well.
5. Gradually add the dry ingredients to the butter mixture and stir until mixed.
6. Mix in the grated carrots and chopped walnuts or pecans if you want to.
7. Pour the batter into the cake pan that has already been greased, and use a spatula to smooth the top.
8. Bake in an oven that has been warm for 30–35 minutes or until a toothpick stuck in the middle comes out clean.
9. After 10 minutes, take the cake from the pan and put it on a wire rack to cool fully.
10. To make cream cheese icing beat together softened cream cheese and melted butter until the mixture is smooth and creamy.
11. Add the powdered sugar slowly while beating until it is well mixed in. Add the vanilla extract and mix well.
12. After the cake has cooled, spread the cream cheese filling all over the top and sides.
13. Cut the Gateau aux Carottes into pieces and serve it.

GÂTEAU DE MAMY (GRANDMA'S CHOCOLATE AND ALMOND CAKE):

INGREDIENTS:
- 1 cup almond flour
- 1/2 cup all-purpose flour
- 1/2 cup unsweetened cocoa powder
- 1/2 teaspoon baking powder
- 1/4 teaspoon salt
- 1 cup unsalted butter, softened
- 1 1/2 cups granulated sugar
- 4 large eggs
- 1 teaspoon vanilla extract
- 1/2 cup milk
- Powdered sugar (for dusting)

INSTRUCTIONS:
1. Set your oven to 350°F (175°C) and turn it on. Coat a round cake pan with butter and flour.
2. Mix the almond flour, all-purpose flour, cocoa powder, baking powder, and salt in a bowl with a whisk.
3. In a separate big bowl, beat the melted butter and powdered sugar until they are light and fluffy.
4. Add the eggs one by one and mix well after each one. Add the vanilla extract and mix well.
5. Alternate adding the dry ingredients and the milk to the butter mixture, starting and ending with the dry ingredients.
6. Pour the batter into the cake pan that has already been greased, and use a spatula to smooth the top.
7. Bake in an oven that has already been warm for 35 to 40 minutes or until a toothpick stuck in the middle comes out clean.
8. After 10 minutes, take the cake from the pan and put it on a wire rack to cool fully.
9. Before you serve the Gateau de Mamy, dust it with powdered sugar.

GÂTEAU FONDANT À L'ORANGE (ORANGE CAKE):

INGREDIENTS:
- 2 cups all-purpose flour
- 1 1/2 teaspoons baking powder
- 1/2 teaspoon baking soda
- 1/2 teaspoon salt
- 1 cup granulated sugar
- 1/2 cup unsalted butter, softened
- 2 large eggs
- 1/2 cup fresh orange juice
- Zest of 2 oranges
- 1/2 cup buttermilk
  For the Orange Glaze:
- 1 cup powdered sugar
- 2-3 tablespoons fresh orange juice

INSTRUCTIONS:
1. Set your oven to 350°F (175°C) and turn it on. Coat a round cake pan with butter and flour.
2. Mix the flour, baking powder, baking soda, and salt in a bowl with a whisk.
3. In a separate big bowl, beat the granulated sugar and melted butter until light and fluffy.
4. Add the eggs one by one and mix well after each one. Mix in the orange peel and fresh orange juice.
5. Add the dry ingredients to the butter mixture slowly, alternating with the buttermilk. Start with the dry ingredients and end with them.
6. Pour the batter into the cake pan that has already been greased, and use a spatula to smooth the top.
7. Bake in an oven that has been warm for 30–35 minutes or until a toothpick stuck in the middle comes out clean.
8. While the cake is baking, make the orange glaze by whisking together the powdered sugar and fresh orange juice until smooth.

9. After 10 minutes, take the cake out of the pan and put it on a wire rack set over a baking sheet.
10. Pour the orange sauce on the hot cake and let it run down the sides.
11. Let the Gateau Fondant à l'Orange cool before you cut it and serve it.

FINANCIER GÉANT (GIANT ALMOND AND BUTTER CAKE):

INGREDIENTS:
- 1 1/2 cups almond flour
- 1 1/2 cups powdered sugar
- 1/2 cup all-purpose flour
- 1/2 teaspoon salt
- 6 large egg whites
- 1 cup unsalted butter, melted
- 1 teaspoon vanilla extract
- Sliced almonds (for topping)

INSTRUCTIONS:
1. Set your oven to 350°F (175°C) and turn it on. Coat a round cake pan with butter and flour.
2. Mix the almond flour, powdered sugar, all-purpose flour, and salt in a bowl with a whisk.
3. Whisk the egg whites in a separate big bowl until they are foamy.
4. Add the dry ingredients to the egg whites slowly until everything is well mixed.
5. Stir the vanilla extract and melted butter into the batter until smooth.
6. Pour the batter into the cake pan that has already been greased, and use a spatula to smooth the top.
7. Sliced nuts should be spread out evenly over the top of the batter.

8. Bake in an oven that has already been warm for 30 to 35 minutes, or until the top is golden brown and a toothpick stuck in the middle comes out clean.
9. After 10 minutes, take the cake from the pan and put it on a wire rack to cool fully.
10. Cut up the Financier Géant and serve it.

CHAPTER:5
COOKIES

FRENCH BUTTER COOKIES (SABLÉS):

INGREDIENTS:

- 1 cup unsalted butter, softened
- 3/4 cup granulated sugar
- 2 large egg yolks
- 2 teaspoons vanilla extract
- 2 cups all-purpose flour
- Pinch of salt
- Demerara sugar (for sprinkling)

INSTRUCTIONS:

1. Cream the warmed butter and granulated sugar until they are light and fluffy.
2. Add the egg whites and vanilla and beat until everything is well mixed.
3. Mix in the flour and salt gradually until the dough comes together.
4. Half the dough and roll each half into a log about 2 inches in diameter.
5. Wrap the logs in plastic wrap and put them in the fridge for at least an hour to chill.
6. Set your oven to 350°F (175°C) and put parchment paper on a baking sheet.
7. Cut the cold dough into pieces that are 1/4 inch thick and put them on the baking sheet that has been prepared.
8. Sprinkle demerara sugar on the cookies.
9. Bake for 12–15 minutes in an oven that has already been warm or until the edges are golden brown.
10. Let the cookies cool for 5 minutes on the baking sheet, then move them to a wire rack to finish cooling.

CHOCOLATE MADELEINES:

INGREDIENTS:
- 3/4 cup all-purpose flour
- 1/4 cup cocoa powder
- 1/2 teaspoon baking powder
- 1/4 teaspoon salt
- 2 large eggs
- 1/2 cup granulated sugar
- 1 teaspoon vanilla extract
- 1/2 cup unsalted butter, melted and cooled
- Powdered sugar (for dusting)

INSTRUCTIONS:
1. Mix the flour, cocoa powder, baking powder, and salt in a bowl with a whisk.
2. Whisk the eggs, sugar, and vanilla extract together in a separate big bowl until they are well mixed.
3. Whisking constantly, slowly add the dry ingredients to the egg mixture until mixed.
4. Pour the melted butter in slowly while whisking. Keep whisking until the batter is smooth.
5. Cover the mixture and put it in the fridge for at least an hour.
6. Set your oven to 375°F (190°C) and grease a madeleine pan.
7. Put about 1 tablespoon of batter into each madeleine shape.
8. Bake in an oven that has already been warm for 8 to 10 minutes, or until the edges are golden brown and the middles bounce back when touched.
9. Put the madeleines out of the pan on a wire rack to cool.
10. Before you serve the Chocolate Madeleines, dust them with powdered sugar.

ORANGE BLOSSOM MACARONS:

INGREDIENTS:

For the Macarons:
- 1 3/4 cups powdered sugar
- 1 cup almond flour
- 3 large egg whites at room temperature
- 1/4 cup granulated sugar
- Orange gel food coloring (optional)

For the Orange Blossom Filling:
- 1/2 cup unsalted butter, softened
- 2 cups powdered sugar
- 1 teaspoon orange blossom water

INSTRUCTIONS:

1. Pulse the powdered sugar and almond flour in a food processor until they are well mixed.
2. Pour the liquid into a big mixing bowl through a fine-mesh sieve.
3. In a separate big mixing bowl, beat the egg whites quickly until they get foamy.
4. Gradually add the granulated sugar while mixing quickly until stiff peaks form.
5. With a spoon, gently fold the powdered sugar and almond flour mixture that has been mixed into the beaten egg whites.
6. If you want, add a few drops of orange gel food coloring and slowly fold them into the batter until they are well mixed.
7. Put the dough into a piping bag with a round tip.
8. Place small rings about 1 inch apart on baking sheets lined with parchment paper.
9. Tap the baking sheets a few times on the counter to get any air bubbles out.
10. Let the piped macarons sit at room temperature for 30 minutes to let a skin form.
11. Set your oven to 300°F (150°C) and turn it on.
12. Bake the macarons in an oven that has already been warm for 15 to 18 minutes or until the tops are set.

13. Before taking the macarons off the baking sheets, let them cool fully.
14. To make the filling, beat together warmed butter, powdered sugar, and orange flower water until smooth.
15. Put a small amount of the orange blossom filling on the flat side of a macaron using a piping bag or a spoon. Then put another macaron on top to make a sandwich.
16. Do the same thing with the rest of the macarons and filling.

PISTACHIO FINANCIERS:

INGREDIENTS:
- 1 cup unsalted butter
- 1 cup powdered sugar
- 1/2 cup almond flour
- 1/2 cup pistachio flour (ground pistachios)
- 1/2 cup all-purpose flour
- 6 large egg whites
- 1/2 teaspoon almond extract
- Chopped pistachios (for garnish)

INSTRUCTIONS:
1. Heat your oven to 375°F (190°C) and grease a financier mold or muffin pan.
2. In a skillet, melt the butter over medium heat until it turns golden brown and smells nutty. Take it off the heat and let it cool down.
3. Mix the powdered sugar, almond flour, pistachio flour, and all-purpose flour in a bowl with a whisk.
4. Whisk the egg whites in a different bowl until they get foamy. Slowly add the egg whites to the dry ingredients and stir until they are mixed.
5. Slowly pour the cooled melted butter and stir in the almond extract until the batter is smooth.
6. Fill about 2/3 of each spot in the financier shape or muffin tin with the batter.

7. On top of each cake, sprinkle chopped pistachios.
8. Bake in an oven that has already been warm for 12 to 15 minutes, or until the edges are golden brown and the middles bounce back when touched.
9. Let the bankers cool for 10 minutes in the mold, then move them to a wire rack to finish cooling.

LAVENDER SHORTBREAD:

INGREDIENTS:
- 1 cup unsalted butter, softened
- 1/2 cup powdered sugar
- 2 cups all-purpose flour
- 1 tablespoon dried lavender buds
- 1/4 teaspoon salt

INSTRUCTIONS:
1. Set your oven to 325°F (165°C) and put parchment paper on a baking sheet.
2. Mix the melted butter and powdered sugar in a bowl until the mixture is light and fluffy.
3. Mix the all-purpose flour, dried lavender buds, and salt separately.
4. Stir the dry ingredients into the butter mixture in a slow, steady stream until a dough forms.
5. Make a ball with the dough and wrap it in plastic wrap. Put in the fridge for at least an hour to cool down.
6. Roll out the cold dough to a thickness of about 1/4 inch on a lightly floured surface.
7. Use a cookie tool to cut out the shapes you want and put them on the baking sheet set up.
8. Bake in an oven that has already been warm for 12 to 15 minutes or until the edges are lightly golden.
9. Let the shortbread cool for 5 minutes on the baking sheet before moving it to a wire rack to cool fully.

FRENCH ALMOND TUILES:

INGREDIENTS:
- 1/2 cup unsalted butter
- 1/2 cup granulated sugar
- 1/4 cup all-purpose flour
- 1/4 cup sliced almonds
- 2 large egg whites
- 1/2 teaspoon vanilla extract

INSTRUCTIONS:
1. Set your oven to 350°F (175°C) and put parchment paper on a baking sheet.
2. Melt the butter in a pot over low heat. Take it off the heat and let it cool down a bit.
3. Mix the powdered sugar, all-purpose flour, and sliced almonds in a bowl with a whisk.
4. Mix the butter that has been melted, the egg whites, and the vanilla extract into the dry ingredients.
5. Drop about 2 inches apart teaspoons of the batter on the baking sheet that has been prepared.
6. Spread each spoonful of batter into a thin, even circle with the back of a spoon.
7. Bake for 8–10 minutes in an oven that has already been warm or until the edges are golden brown.
8. Take the tiles off the baking sheet and shape them immediately while they are still hot and malleable. You can bend them into curves or roll them into tubes.
9. Let the tiles cool down on a wire rack.

CHOCOLATE-DIPPED PALMIERS:

INGREDIENTS:

- 1 sheet puff pastry, thawed
- 1/2 cup granulated sugar
- 1 tablespoon unsweetened cocoa powder
- 1/4 teaspoon ground cinnamon
- 4 ounces semi-sweet chocolate, chopped
- 1 tablespoon vegetable oil

INSTRUCTIONS:

1. Set your oven to 400°F (200°C) and put parchment paper on a baking sheet.
2. Mix the sugar, cocoa powder, and cinnamon in a small bowl with a whisk.
3. Half the sugar mixture should be spread evenly on a clean surface.
4. Fold the sheet of thawed puff pastry over the sugar mixture, and then put the rest of the sugar mixture on top.
5. Roll the puff pastry into a 12x10-inch square with a rolling pin.
6. Roll each end of the puff pastry toward the middle, starting from the longer side. They should meet in the middle.
7. Cut the rolled puff pastry into pieces that are 1/2 inch thick and place them on the baking sheet that has been prepared.
8. Bake the palmiers in an oven that has already been hot for 15 to 20 minutes or until golden brown and crisp.
9. Put the palmiers off the baking sheet on a wire rack to cool fully.
10. Mix the chopped semisweet chocolate and vegetable oil in a bowl that can go in the microwave.
11. After each short time, stir the chocolate in the microwave until it is melted and smooth.
12. Dip one end of each palmier that has cooled off into the melted chocolate and let the extra chocolate drip off.
13. Put the palmiers dipped in chocolate on parchment paper or a wire rack to set the chocolate.

NUTELLA STUFFED COOKIES:

INGREDIENTS:
- 1 cup unsalted butter, softened
- 1 cup granulated sugar
- 1 cup packed brown sugar
- 2 large eggs
- 1 teaspoon vanilla extract
- 3 cups all-purpose flour
- 1/2 teaspoon baking soda
- 1/2 teaspoon salt
- Nutella (for filling)

INSTRUCTIONS:
1. Set your oven to 350°F (175°C) and put parchment paper on a baking sheet.
2. Cream the melted butter, white sugar, and brown sugar in a bowl until light and fluffy.
3. Add the eggs one by one and mix well after each one. Add the vanilla extract and mix well.
4. Mix the all-purpose flour, baking soda, and salt separately.
5. Gradually add the dry ingredients to the butter mixture and stir until mixed.
6. Flatten out about 1 tablespoon of cookie dough in the palm of your hand.
7. Put a small amount of Nutella in the middle of the dough that has been pressed.
8. Fold the dough around the Nutella to seal it inside the dough.
9. Make sure all of the Nutella is spread by rolling the dough into a ball.
10. Place the cookie dough balls on the baking sheet, leaving about 2 inches between each.
11. Bake for 10–12 minutes in an oven that has already been warm or until the edges are golden brown.
12. Let the cookies cool for 5 minutes on the baking sheet, then move them to a wire rack to finish cooling.

FRENCH SPICE COOKIES (PAIN D'ÉPICES):

INGREDIENTS:
- 2 cups all-purpose flour
- 1/2 cup honey
- 1/2 cup molasses
- 1/2 cup granulated sugar
- 1/2 cup unsalted butter, melted
- 2 teaspoons ground cinnamon
- 1/2 teaspoon ground ginger
- 1/4 teaspoon ground cloves
- 1/4 teaspoon ground nutmeg
- 1/4 teaspoon ground cardamom
- 1/4 teaspoon salt
- 2 teaspoons baking powder
- 1/2 cup milk

INSTRUCTIONS:
1. Set your oven to 325°F (165°C) and put parchment paper on a baking sheet.
2. Mix the all-purpose flour, ground cinnamon, ginger, ground cloves, ground nutmeg, ground cardamom, salt, and baking powder in a bowl.
3. Mix the honey, molasses, granulated sugar, melted butter, and milk together in a separate big bowl until everything is well mixed.
4. Slowly add the dry ingredients to the wet ingredients and stir until they are mixed.
5. Put about 2 inches between each tablespoon of cookie dough on the baking sheet that has been prepared.
6. Bake the cookies in an oven that has been warm for 12 to 15 minutes or until they are set and have a light brown color.
7. Let the cookies cool for 5 minutes on the baking sheet, then move them to a wire rack to finish cooling.

CHOCOLATE HAZELNUT MACARONS:

INGREDIENTS:

For the Macarons:
- 1 3/4 cups powdered sugar
- 1 cup almond flour
- 3 large egg whites at room temperature
- 1/4 cup granulated sugar
- 1/4 cup unsweetened cocoa powder
- Hazelnut spread (such as Nutella)

For the Chocolate Ganache:
- 4 ounces semi-sweet chocolate, chopped
- 1/2 cup heavy cream
- 1 tablespoon unsalted butter

INSTRUCTIONS:

1. Pulse the powdered sugar, almond flour, and chocolate powder in a food processor until they are well mixed.
2. Pour the mixture into a big mixing bowl through a fine-mesh sieve.
3. In a separate big mixing bowl, beat the egg whites quickly until they get foamy.
4. Gradually add the granulated sugar while mixing quickly until stiff peaks form.
5. Use a spatula to gently fold the powdered sugar, almond flour, and cocoa mixture that has been mixed into the beaten egg whites.
6. Put the dough into a piping bag with a round tip.
7. Place small rings about 1 inch apart on baking sheets lined with parchment paper.
8. Tap the baking sheets a few times on the counter to get any air bubbles out.
9. Let the piped macarons sit at room temperature for 30 minutes to let a skin form.
10. Set your oven to 300°F (150°C) and turn it on.

11. Bake the macarons in an oven that has already been warm for 15 to 18 minutes or until the tops are set.
12. Before taking the macarons off the baking sheets, let them cool fully.
13. Put the chopped semisweet chocolate in a heat-safe bowl to make the chocolate sauce.
14. Heat the heavy cream in a pot until it just starts to bubble. Pour the hot cream over the pieces of chocolate and let it sit for a minute.
15. Add the unsalted butter to the bowl and whisk the mixture until the chocolate has melted and the ganache is smooth.
16. Let the ganache cool until it gets just a little bit thicker.
17. Spread some hazelnut spread on the flat side of one macaron, then put another macaron on top.
18. Repeat with the rest of the macarons, filling them with the chocolate ganache.

RASPBERRY FILLED FRENCH BUTTER COOKIES:

INGREDIENTS:

For the Cookies:
- 1 cup unsalted butter, softened
- 1/2 cup powdered sugar
- 2 cups all-purpose flour
- 1/2 teaspoon salt
- 1 teaspoon vanilla extract
- Raspberry jam (for filling)

For the Glaze:
- 1 cup powdered sugar
- 1-2 tablespoons milk
- 1/2 teaspoon vanilla extract

INSTRUCTIONS:

1. Set your oven to 350°F (175°C) and put parchment paper on a baking sheet.

2. Mix the melted butter and powdered sugar in a bowl until the mixture is light and fluffy.
3. Add the all-purpose flour, salt, and vanilla extract to the butter mixture and stir until a soft dough forms.
4. Roll the dough into small balls that are about 1 inch across.
5. Put the dough balls on the baking sheet, leaving about 2 inches between each.
6. Make a hole in the middle of each dough ball with your thumb or the end of a wooden spoon.
7. Put a small amount of raspberry jam into each hole.
8. Bake in an oven that has already been warm for 12 to 15 minutes or until the edges are lightly golden.
9. Let the cookies cool for 5 minutes on the baking sheet, then move them to a wire rack to finish cooling.
10. Mix the powdered sugar, milk, and vanilla extract until smooth.
11. Pour the sauce over the cookies after they have cooled.
12. Let the glaze set before you serve the Raspberry Filled French Butter Cookies.

LEMON MADELEINES:

INGREDIENTS:
- 2/3 cup all-purpose flour
- 1/2 teaspoon baking powder
- Pinch of salt
- 1/2 cup granulated sugar
- Zest of 1 lemon
- 2 large eggs
- 1/2 teaspoon vanilla extract
- 6 tablespoons unsalted butter, melted and cooled
- Powdered sugar (for dusting)

INSTRUCTIONS:
1. Mix the all-purpose flour, baking powder, and salt in a bowl with a whisk.

2. Mix the granulated sugar and lemon juice in a separate large bowl. Use your fingers to rub the lemon peel into the sugar to get the oils out.
3. Whisk the eggs into the sugar mixture until they are well mixed in.
4. Add the vanilla extract and mix well.
5. Add the dry ingredients to the egg mixture a little, stirring until they are mixed in.
6. Fold the melted butter into the batter slowly until it is smooth.
7. Cover the mixture and put it in the fridge for at least an hour.
8. Set your oven to 375°F (190°C) and grease a madeleine pan.
9. Put about 1 tablespoon of batter into each madeleine shape.
10. Bake for 10–12 minutes in an oven that has already been heated or until the edges are golden brown and the cores bounce back when touched.
11. Put the madeleines out of the pan on a wire rack to cool.
12. Before you serve the Lemon Madeleines, dust them with powdered sugar.

PECAN SANDIES:

INGREDIENTS:
- 1 cup unsalted butter, softened
- 1/2 cup powdered sugar
- 2 cups all-purpose flour
- 1/2 teaspoon salt
- 1 teaspoon vanilla extract
- 1 cup finely chopped pecans

INSTRUCTIONS:
1. Set your oven to 350°F (175°C) and put parchment paper on a baking sheet.
2. Mix the melted butter and powdered sugar in a bowl until the mixture is light and fluffy.

3. Add the all-purpose flour, salt, and vanilla extract to the butter mixture and stir until a lumpy dough forms.
4. Add the finely chopped nuts and stir until everything is well-mixed.
5. Roll the dough into small balls that are about an inch across.
6. Put the dough balls on the baking sheet, leaving about 2 inches between each.
7. Flatten each dough ball into a disk shape with the bottom of a glass or the palm of your hand.
8. Bake in an oven that has already been warm for 12 to 15 minutes or until the edges are lightly golden.
9. Let the cookies cool for 5 minutes on the baking sheet, then move them to a wire rack to finish cooling.

SALTED CARAMEL MACARONS:

INGREDIENTS:
For the Macarons:
- 1 3/4 cups powdered sugar
- 1 cup almond flour
- 3 large egg whites at room temperature
- 1/4 cup granulated sugar
- 1/2 teaspoon salt
- Caramel sauce (for filling)
For the Salted Caramel Filling:
- 1/2 cup granulated sugar
- 2 tablespoons water
- 1/4 cup heavy cream
- 2 tablespoons unsalted butter
- 1/4 teaspoon sea salt

INSTRUCTIONS:
1. Pulse the powdered sugar and almond flour in a food processor until they are well mixed.
2. Pour the mixture into a big mixing bowl through a fine-mesh sieve.

3. In a separate big mixing bowl, beat the egg whites quickly until they get foamy.
4. Add the sugar and salt slowly while beating quickly until stiff peaks form.
5. With a spatula, gently fold the powdered sugar and almond flour mixture that has been mixed into the beaten egg whites.
6. Put the dough into a piping bag with a round tip.
7. Place small rings about 1 inch apart on baking sheets lined with parchment paper.
8. Tap the baking sheets a few times on the counter to get any air bubbles out.
9. Let the piped macarons sit at room temperature for 30 minutes to let a skin form.
10. Set your oven to 300°F (150°C) and turn it on.
11. Bake the macarons in an oven that has already been warm for 15 to 18 minutes or until the tops are set.
12. Before taking the macarons off the baking sheets, let them cool fully.
13. Mix the powdered sugar and water in a saucepan over medium heat to fill the salted caramel. Stir until all of the sugar is gone.
14. Turn the heat up to high and cook the mixture without moving until it turns a deep amber color.
15. Take the pan off the heat and slowly pour in the heavy cream. Be careful because the mixture will start to bubble.
16. Back on low heat, add the unsalted butter and sea salt while whisking until the caramel is smooth.
17. Let it cool down all the way.
18. Put a small amount of the salted caramel filling on the flat side of a macaron using a piping bag or a spoon. Then put another macaron on top to make a sandwich.
19. Do the same thing with the rest of the macarons and filling.

CHOCOLATE FRENCH SABLE COOKIES:

INGREDIENTS:
- 1 1/4 cups all-purpose flour
- 1/4 cup unsweetened cocoa powder
- 1/4 teaspoon salt
- 1/2 cup unsalted butter, softened
- 1/2 cup powdered sugar
- 1 large egg yolk
- 1 teaspoon vanilla extract
- Melted chocolate for drizzling (optional)

INSTRUCTIONS:
1. Mix the all-purpose flour, cocoa powder, and salt in a bowl with a whisk.
2. In a separate big bowl, beat the softened butter and powdered sugar until light and fluffy.
3. Mix the egg yolk and vanilla extract into the butter mixture while beating.
4. Mix the dry ingredients into the butter mixture, stirring until the dough comes together.
5. Make a ball with the dough, wrap it in plastic wrap, and put it in the fridge for at least an hour.
6. Set your oven to 325°F (165°C) and put parchment paper on a baking sheet.
7. Roll out the cold dough to a thickness of about 1/4 inch on a lightly floured surface.
8. Use a cookie tool to cut out the shapes you want and put them on the baking sheet set up.
9. Use a fork to poke holes in the top of each cookie to make a design.
10. Bake for 12–15 minutes in an oven that has already been warm or until the edges are firm.
11. Let the cookies cool for 5 minutes on the baking sheet, then move them to a wire rack to finish cooling.

12. If you want, you can drizzle melted chocolate over the cookies after they have cooled. Wait until the chocolate is set to serve it.

CHAPTER:6
BAKED DESSERTS

CLAFOUTIS AUX CERISES (CHERRY CLAFOUTIS):

INGREDIENTS:
- 1 cup cherries, pitted
- 2/3 cup all-purpose flour
- 1/2 cup granulated sugar
- 1/4 teaspoon salt
- 3 large eggs
- 1 cup milk
- 1 teaspoon vanilla extract
- Powdered sugar (for dusting)

INSTRUCTIONS:
1. Set your oven to 350°F (175°C) and grease a baking dish.
2. Put a single layer of the pitted cherries in the prepared baking dish.
3. Mix the all-purpose flour, sugar, and salt in a bowl with a whisk.
4. Beat the eggs in a different bowl. Add the milk and vanilla extract slowly, beating until everything is well mixed.
5. Mix the dry ingredients slowly while stirring the egg mixture until a smooth batter forms.
6. Put the cherries in a baking dish and pour the batter over them.

7. Bake the clafoutis in an oven that has already been warm for 35 to 40 minutes, or until the top is set and golden brown.
8. Take the clafoutis out of the oven and let it cool down for a few minutes.
9. Before you serve the clafoutis, dust it with powdered sugar.

TARTE TATIN (CARAMELIZED APPLE TART):

INGREDIENTS:
- 6-8 apples, peeled, cored, and halved
- 1/2 cup unsalted butter
- 1 cup granulated sugar
- 1 teaspoon vanilla extract
- 1 sheet puff pastry, thawed

INSTRUCTIONS:
1. Set your oven to 375°F (190°C) to get it ready.
2. Melt the butter in a dish or pan that can go in the oven.
3. Stir the sugar into the hot butter until it is all dissolved.
4. Add the vanilla extract and mix well.
5. Put the cut side down of the apple halves in a circle in the pan.
6. Cook the apples in the caramel mixture for about 10 minutes, or until they soften and the caramel turns golden brown.
7. Take the pan off the heat.
8. Put the puff pastry sheet on top of the apples that have been caramelized, and tuck the sides down into the skillet.
9. Bake for 20–25 minutes in an oven that has already been warmed or until the pastry is golden brown.
10. Take the tart out of the oven carefully and let it cool down for a few minutes.
11. Place a serving plate or platter over the skillet, and then slowly flip the skillet over to get the tart onto the plate.
12. The Tarte Tatin can be served hot or at room temperature.

GÂTEAU BASQUE (BASQUE CAKE):

INGREDIENTS:

For the Dough:
- 2 cups all-purpose flour
- 3/4 cup unsalted butter, softened
- 1 cup granulated sugar
- 3 large egg yolks
- 1/4 teaspoon salt
- 1 teaspoon vanilla extract
- 1/2 teaspoon almond extract
- Zest of 1 lemon

For the Filling:
- 1 cup pastry cream or thick custard
- 1/2 cup cherry jam or preserves (optional)

INSTRUCTIONS:

1. Cream the warmed butter and granulated sugar until they are light and fluffy.
2. Add the egg yolks one at a time, beating well after each. Mix in the extracts of vanilla, almond, and lemon.
3. Mix the all-purpose flour and salt into the butter mixture in small amounts, stirring until a dough forms.
4. Split the dough into two pieces that are the same size.
5. Press one piece of dough evenly into the bottom of a cake pan that has been greased.
6. Spread the pastry cream or thick custard over the dough in the pan. Spread cherry jam or preserves on top of the pastry cream if you want to.
7. Roll out the rest of the dough and put it on the filling. Seal the sides by pressing them together.
8. Bake at 350°F (175°C) in an oven that has already been warm for 25 to 30 minutes or until the cake is golden brown.
9. Take the cake out of the oven and let it cool for a few minutes in the pan before moving it to a wire rack to finish cooling.

BRIOCHE BREAD PUDDING:

INGREDIENTS:
- 4 cups brioche bread, cut into cubes
- 3 cups whole milk
- 4 large eggs
- 1/2 cup granulated sugar
- 1 teaspoon vanilla extract
- 1/2 teaspoon ground cinnamon
- 1/4 teaspoon ground nutmeg
- Pinch of salt
- 1/2 cup raisins (optional)
- Powdered sugar (for dusting)

INSTRUCTIONS:
1. Set your oven to 350°F (175°C) and grease a baking dish.
2. Mix the milk, eggs, sugar, vanilla extract, ground cinnamon, ground nutmeg, and salt in a big bowl with a whisk.
3. Add the cubes of brioche bread and raisins, if you're using them, to the milk mixture and stir until the bread is thoroughly soaked and coated.
4. Let the ingredients sit together for about 15 minutes so the bread can soak up the liquid.
5. Spread the bread pudding mixture evenly in the baking dish that has been greased.
6. Bake the bread pudding in an oven that has already been warm for 45 to 50 minutes or until the top is set and golden brown.
7. Take the bread pudding out of the oven and let it cool down for a few minutes.
8. Before you serve the bread pudding, dust it with powdered sugar.

PEARS POACHED IN RED WINE:

INGREDIENTS:

- 4-6 firm pears, peeled and cored
- 1 bottle of red wine
- 1 cup granulated sugar
- 1 cinnamon stick
- 2 cloves
- Zest of 1 orange

INSTRUCTIONS:

1. Mix the red wine, sugar, cinnamon stick, cloves, and orange zest in a big saucepan.
2. Over medium heat, bring the mixture to a boil while stirring until the sugar is dissolved.
3. Add the peeled and cored pears to the liquid already heating up.
4. Turn the heat down to low and poach the pears for about 30 minutes or until they are soft and easily poked with a fork.
5. Take the pears out of the juice and let them cool down.
6. Serve the pears warm or cold with a drizzle of the liquid used to cook them.

GÂTEAU AU YAOURT (FRENCH YOGURT CAKE):

INGREDIENTS:

- 1 cup plain yogurt
- 1 cup granulated sugar
- 3 large eggs
- 1/2 cup vegetable oil
- 2 cups all-purpose flour
- 2 teaspoons baking powder
- 1/2 teaspoon salt
- Zest of 1 lemon

- Powdered sugar (for dusting)

INSTRUCTIONS:

1. Set your oven to 350°F (175°C) and grease a cake pan.
2. Whisk the plain yogurt, powdered sugar, eggs, and vegetable oil together until everything is well-mixed.
3. Mix the all-purpose flour, baking powder, salt, and lemon juice separately.
4. Mix the dry ingredients slowly while stirring the yogurt mixture until you have a smooth batter.
5. Spread the batter out evenly in the greased cake pan and pour in the batter.
6. Bake the cake in an oven that has already been heated for 30 to 35 minutes or until it is golden brown and a toothpick placed in the middle comes out clean.
7. Take the cake out of the oven and let it cool for a few minutes in the pan before moving it to a wire rack to finish cooling.
8. Before you serve the Gateau au Yaourt, dust it with powdered sugar.

CHOCOLATE SOUFFLÉ:

INGREDIENTS:

- 4 ounces bittersweet chocolate, chopped
- 3 tablespoons unsalted butter
- 1/3 cup granulated sugar divided
- 4 large eggs separated
- 1/4 teaspoon cream of tartar
- Powdered sugar (for dusting)

INSTRUCTIONS:

1. Set your oven to 375°F (190°C) to get it ready. Grease each ramekin, coat it with powdered sugar and tap off any extra.
2. Melt the chopped bittersweet chocolate and unsalted butter in a bowl that can handle heat over a double boiler. Stir the mixture until it is smooth. Take it off the heat and let it cool down a bit.

3. Beat the egg whites with half of the granulated sugar in a bowl until the mixture is thick and pale yellow.
4. Whisk the chocolate mixture slowly into the egg yolk mixture until everything is well mixed.
5. In a different bowl, beat the egg whites and cream of tartar together until they become foamy. Add the remaining granulated sugar slowly while beating until stiff peaks form.
6. To make the chocolate mixture lighter, gently fold one-third of the beaten egg whites. Then, gently fold in the rest of the egg whites until there are no more streaks.
7. Pour about three-quarters of the soufflé mixture into each of the ramekins that have been prepped.
8. Place the ramekins on a baking sheet and bake in a warm oven for 12 to 15 minutes or until the soufflés are set.
9. Take the soufflés out of the oven and sprinkle powdered sugar on them.
10. Serve the Chocolate Soufflés right away because they will quickly lose their shape.

FRENCH APPLE CAKE:

INGREDIENTS:
- 3 medium apples, peeled, cored, and thinly sliced
- 2 tablespoons unsalted butter, melted
- 1 cup all-purpose flour
- 1 teaspoon baking powder
- 1/4 teaspoon salt
- 1/2 cup granulated sugar
- 2 large eggs
- 1/2 cup milk
- 1 teaspoon vanilla extract
- Powdered sugar (for dusting)

INSTRUCTIONS:
1. Set your oven to 350°F (175°C) and grease a cake pan.

2. Mix the thinly sliced apples and melted butter in a bowl until the apples are covered.
3. Mix the all-purpose flour, baking powder, salt, and granulated sugar in a separate bowl.
4. Beat the eggs in another bowl. Mix the milk and vanilla flavor with a whisk.
5. Mix the dry ingredients slowly while stirring the egg mixture until a smooth batter forms.
6. Pour half of the batter into a cake pan that has been greased.
7. Place the apple slices in a single layer on top of the batter.
8. Spread the rest of the batter evenly on top of the apples.
9. Bake the cake in an oven that has already been heated for 30 to 35 minutes or until it is golden brown and a toothpick placed in the middle comes out clean.
10. Take the cake out of the oven and let it cool for a few minutes in the pan before moving it to a wire rack to finish cooling.
11. Before serving, the French Apple Cake is dusted with powdered sugar.

RASPBERRY FRANGIPANE TART:

INGREDIENTS:

For the Tart Crust:
- 1 1/4 cups all-purpose flour
- 1/4 cup granulated sugar
- 1/4 teaspoon salt
- 1/2 cup unsalted butter, cold and cut into small pieces
- 1 large egg yolk
- 1 tablespoon ice water

For the Frangipane Filling:
- 1/2 cup almond flour
- 1/4 cup granulated sugar
- 1/4 cup unsalted butter, softened
- 1 large egg
- 1/2 teaspoon vanilla extract

For the Topping:

- Fresh raspberries
- Powdered sugar (for dusting)

INSTRUCTIONS:

1. Set your oven to 375°F (190°C) and grease a tart pan.
2. Mix the all-purpose flour, sugar, and salt in a food processor. Mix by pulsing a few times.
3. Add the cold butter to the food processor and pulse until the mixture resembles coarse bits.
4. Whisk the egg yolk and ice water together in a small bowl. Add this to the food processor and pulse until the dough comes together.
5. Move the dough to a lightly floured surface and shape it into a ball. Cover with plastic wrap and put in the fridge for at least 30 minutes.
6. Roll out the cold dough into a circle big enough to fit your tart pan on a lightly floured surface. Press the dough into a tart pan that has been greased, and cut off any extra dough.
7. Cream the almond flour, granulated sugar, melted butter, egg, and vanilla extract until everything is well mixed.
8. Spread the frangipane filling out evenly on the tart crust's bottom.
9. Place fresh strawberries on the frangipane filling and gently press them into it.
10. Bake for 25 to 30 minutes in an oven that has already been heated or until the top is golden brown and the frangipane is set.
11. Take the tart out of the oven and let it cool for a few minutes in the pan before moving it to a wire rack to finish cooling.
12. Before it is served, the Raspberry Frangipane Tart is dusted with powdered sugar.

CHERRY AND ALMOND GALETTE:

INGREDIENTS:

For the Galette Dough:
- 1 1/4 cups all-purpose flour
- 1 tablespoon granulated sugar
- 1/4 teaspoon salt
- 1/2 cup unsalted butter, cold and cut into small pieces
- 1/4 cup ice water

For the Filling:
- 2 cups fresh cherries, pitted
- 2 tablespoons granulated sugar
- 1 tablespoon cornstarch
- 1/2 teaspoon almond extract

For the Glaze:
- 1 large egg, beaten
- Coarse sugar (for sprinkling)

INSTRUCTIONS:

1. Set your oven to 375°F (190°C) and put parchment paper on a baking sheet.
2. Mix the all-purpose flour, sugar, and salt in a food processor. Mix by pulsing a few times.
3. Add the cold butter to the food processor and pulse until the mixture resembles coarse bits.
4. Gradually add the ice water to the food processor and pulse until the dough comes together.
5. Move the dough to a lightly floured surface and shape it into a ball. Cover with plastic wrap and put in the fridge for at least 30 minutes.
6. Mix the cherries with the granulated sugar, cornstarch, and almond flavor in a bowl. Toss the plums until they are well covered.
7. Roll out the cold dough into a circle about 12 inches in diameter on a lightly floured surface.
8. Move the rolled-out dough to the baking sheet that has been prepped.

9. Spoon the cherry filling into the middle of the dough, leaving a border around the sides.
10. To make a rustic galette shape, fold the dough sides over the filling and pleat as needed.
11. Brush the sides of the dough with beaten egg, then sprinkle coarse sugar over the edges and the cherry filling.
12. Bake for 25 to 30 minutes in an oven that has already been heated or until the crust is golden brown and the cherry sauce is bubbling.
13. Take the galette out of the oven and let it cool for a few minutes on the baking sheet before moving it to a wire rack to cool all the way.

CARAMELIZED PEACH TART:

INGREDIENTS:

For the Tart Crust:
- 1 1/4 cups all-purpose flour
- 1/4 cup granulated sugar
- 1/4 teaspoon salt
- 1/2 cup unsalted butter, cold and cut into small pieces
- 1 large egg yolk
- 1 tablespoon ice water

For the Peach Filling:
- 4-5 peaches, peeled, pitted, and sliced
- 1/4 cup granulated sugar
- 1 tablespoon cornstarch
- 1/2 teaspoon vanilla extract
- 1/4 teaspoon ground cinnamon

For the Caramel Sauce:
- 1/2 cup granulated sugar
- 1/4 cup heavy cream
- 2 tablespoons unsalted butter
- Pinch of salt

INSTRUCTIONS:

1. Set your oven to 375°F (190°C) and grease a tart pan.
2. Mix the all-purpose flour, sugar, and salt in a food processor. Mix by pulsing a few times.
3. Add the cold butter to the food processor and pulse until the mixture resembles coarse bits.
4. Whisk the egg yolk and ice water together in a small bowl. Add this to the food processor and pulse until the dough comes together.
5. Move the dough to a lightly floured surface and shape it into a ball. Cover with plastic wrap and put in the fridge for at least 30 minutes.
6. Roll out the cold dough into a circle big enough to fit your tart pan on a lightly floured surface. Press the dough into a tart pan that has been greased, and cut off any extra dough.
7. Mix the sliced peaches with the sugar, cornstarch, vanilla extract, and ground cinnamon until well-covered.
8. Make an even layer of peach slices on top of the tart crust.
9. In a small saucepan, melt the granulated sugar over medium heat until it turns light brown.
10. Turn off the heat and carefully add the heavy cream, unsalted butter, and salt to the pan. Mix the caramel sauce until it is smooth.
11. The caramel sauce should be drizzled over the peaches in the tart.
12. Bake for 30–35 minutes in an oven that has already been warm or until the crust is golden brown and the peaches are soft.
13. Take the tart out of the oven and let it cool for a few minutes in the pan before moving it to a wire rack to finish cooling.

CHOCOLATE LAVA CAKE (MOELLEUX AU CHOCOLAT):

INGREDIENTS:

- 4 ounces bittersweet chocolate, chopped
- 1/2 cup unsalted butter
- 2 large eggs
- 2 large egg yolks
- 1/4 cup granulated sugar
- 2 tablespoons all-purpose flour
- Powdered sugar (for dusting)
- Fresh berries (for garnish)

INSTRUCTIONS:

1. Set your oven to 425°F (220°C) and turn it on. Grease each ramekin, fill it with cocoa powder or granulated sugar and tap off any extra.
2. Melt the chopped bittersweet chocolate and unsalted butter in a bowl that can handle heat over a double boiler. Stir the mixture until it is smooth. Take it off the heat and let it cool down a bit.
3. Beat the eggs, egg whites, and granulated sugar until the mixture is thick and pale yellow.
4. Whisk the melting chocolate mixture into the egg mixture in small amounts until everything is well mixed.
5. Sift the all-purpose flour over the chocolate mixture and fold it gently until there are no more streaks.
6. Pour about three-quarters of the batter into each of the ramekins that have been prepped.
7. Place the ramekins on a baking sheet and bake in the warm oven for 10 to 12 minutes, or until the edges are set, but the centers are still soft.
8. Take the ramekins out of the oven and give them a few minutes to cool down.
9. Turn each ramekin upside down onto a serving plate and carefully remove it to show the molten chocolate in the middle.

10. Before serving, sprinkle the Chocolate Lava Cakes with powdered sugar and top them with fresh berries.

FRENCH ALMOND CAKE:

INGREDIENTS:
- 1 cup almond flour
- 1/2 cup all-purpose flour
- 1 teaspoon baking powder
- 1/4 teaspoon salt
- 1/2 cup unsalted butter, softened
- 1 cup granulated sugar
- 3 large eggs
- 1 teaspoon vanilla extract
- 1/2 teaspoon almond extract
- Sliced almonds (for garnish)
- Powdered sugar (for dusting)

INSTRUCTIONS:
1. Set your oven to 350°F (175°C) and grease a cake pan.
2. Mix the almond flour, all-purpose flour, baking powder, and salt in a bowl with a whisk.
3. In a separate big bowl, beat the softened butter and granulated sugar until they are light and fluffy.
4. Add the eggs one by one and mix well after each one. Mix in the extracts of vanilla and almonds.
5. Mix the dry ingredients slowly while stirring the butter mixture until a smooth batter forms.
6. Spread the batter out evenly in the greased cake pan and pour in the batter.
7. Sliced nuts should be put on top of the batter.
8. Bake the cake in an oven that has already been heated for 30 to 35 minutes or until it is golden brown and a toothpick placed in the middle comes out clean.
9. Take the cake out of the oven and let it cool for a few minutes in the pan before moving it to a wire rack to finish cooling.

10. Powdered sugar is sprinkled on top of the French Almond Cake before it is served.

BERRY GRATIN WITH CHAMPAGNE SABAYON:

INGREDIENTS:

For the Berry Gratin:
- Mixed berries (such as strawberries, raspberries, and blueberries)
- 1/4 cup granulated sugar
- 1 tablespoon lemon juice
- Zest of 1 lemon

For the Champagne Sabayon:
- 4 large egg yolks
- 1/4 cup granulated sugar
- 1/2 cup champagne or sparkling wine
- Fresh mint leaves (for garnish)

INSTRUCTIONS:

1. Set your oven to broil and heat it.
2. Mix the mixed berries, granulated sugar, lemon juice, and lemon zest in a bowl. Toss the berries until they are well covered.
3. Spread the berry mixture out in a single layer in a baking dish.
4. Put the baking dish under the grill and cook for 3–5 minutes, or until the berries release their juices and the sugar caramelize. Keep an eye on them so they don't catch fire.
5. Make the champagne sabayon while the berries are cooking. Whisk the egg whites and granulated sugar in a bowl that can handle heat until well mixed.
6. Place the bowl over a pan of boiling water, making sure the bottom of the bowl doesn't touch the water. Whisk the champagne or sparkling wine in slowly.

7. Whisk the mixture over the boiling water until it thickens and forms a ribbon when the whisk is lifted.
8. Take the bowl off the stove and let the sabayon cool down slightly.
9. To serve, put a spoonful of the warm, sautéed berries in each dish and add a dollop of champagne sabayon on top.
10. Before serving, sprinkle with fresh mint leaves.

LEMON MADELEINES:

INGREDIENTS:

- 2/3 cup all-purpose flour
- 1/2 teaspoon baking powder
- 1/4 teaspoon salt
- 2 large eggs
- 1/2 cup granulated sugar
- 1 teaspoon lemon zest
- 1 tablespoon lemon juice
- 1/2 teaspoon vanilla extract
- 6 tablespoons unsalted butter, melted and cooled
- Powdered sugar (for dusting)

INSTRUCTIONS:

1. Heat your oven to 375°F (190°C), grease madeleine pans, or a madeleine pan.
2. Mix the all-purpose flour, baking powder, and salt in a bowl with a whisk.
3. In a separate big bowl, beat the eggs, granulated sugar, lemon zest, lemon juice, and vanilla extract until the mixture is thick and pale yellow.
4. Add the dry ingredients to the egg mixture gradually and stir until everything is well mixed.
5. Slowly pour the melted butter and gently fold it in until it is all mixed in.
6. Put about three-quarters of the batter into each greased madeleine shape.

7. Bake the madeleines in an oven that has been warm for 10 to 12 minutes or until the edges are golden and bounce back when lightly touched.
8. Take the madeleines out of the oven and let them cool for a few minutes in the molds before putting them on a wire rack to cool fully.
9. Before serving, dust the Lemon Madeleines with powdered sugar.

PUMPKIN CRÈME BRÛLÉE:

INGREDIENTS:
- 1 cup heavy cream
- 1 cup canned pumpkin puree
- 1/2 teaspoon vanilla extract
- 1/2 teaspoon ground cinnamon
- 1/4 teaspoon ground nutmeg
- 1/8 teaspoon ground ginger
- 4 large egg yolks
- 1/2 cup granulated sugar, plus extra for caramelizing

INSTRUCTIONS:
1. Put 4-6 ramekins in a baking dish and heat the oven to 325°F (160°C).
2. ·Heavy cream, canned pumpkin puree, vanilla extract, ground cinnamon, ground nutmeg, and ground ginger are heated over medium heat in a pot until it starts to steam. Do not let it boil.
3. Whisk the egg whites and granulated sugar together in a different bowl until they are well mixed.
4. Slowly pour the hot cream mixture into the egg yolk mixture as you whisk.
5. Divide the mixture between the ramekins in the baking dish in an even way.

6. Put the baking dish in the oven that has already been heated, and slowly pour hot water around the ramekins to make a water bath.
7. Bake for 30–35 minutes, or until the sides of the custards are set, but the middle is still slightly loose.
8. Take the dish out of the oven and cool the custards in the water bath. Once the ramekins have cooled, take them out of the water bath and put them in the fridge for at least 2 hours or until they are cold and set.
9. Sprinkle white sugar evenly over the top of each custard right before serving. Use a kitchen torch to heat the sugar until it turns golden brown and makes a crust.
10. Let the Pumpkin Crème Brûlée sit for a minute or two before serving so that the sugar can harden.

NORMANDY APPLE TART:

INGREDIENTS:
For the Tart Crust:
- 1 1/4 cups all-purpose flour
- 1/4 cup granulated sugar
- 1/4 teaspoon salt
- 1/2 cup unsalted butter, cold and cut into small pieces
- 1 large egg yolk
- 1 tablespoon ice water

For the Apple Filling:
- 4-5 apples, peeled, cored, and thinly sliced
- 1/4 cup granulated sugar
- 1 tablespoon lemon juice
- 1/4 teaspoon ground cinnamon

For the Crumble Topping:
- 1/2 cup all-purpose flour
- 1/4 cup granulated sugar
- 1/4 cup unsalted butter, cold and cut into small pieces

INSTRUCTIONS:

1. Set your oven to 375°F (190°C) and grease a tart pan.
2. Mix the all-purpose flour, sugar, and salt in a food processor. Mix by pulsing a few times.
3. Add the cold butter to the food processor and pulse until the mixture resembles coarse bits.
4. Whisk the egg yolk and ice water together in a small bowl. Add this to the food processor and pulse until the dough comes together.
5. Move the dough to a lightly floured surface and shape it into a ball. Cover with plastic wrap and put in the fridge for at least 30 minutes.
6. Roll out the cold dough into a circle big enough to fit your tart pan on a lightly floured surface. Press the dough into a tart pan that has been greased, and cut off any extra dough.
7. Mix the powdered sugar, lemon juice, and ground cinnamon with the thinly sliced apples in a bowl until the apples are well-covered.
8. Make an even layer of apple slices on top of the tart crust.
9. Mix all-purpose flour, granulated sugar, and cold butter in a separate bowl for the crumble topping. Cut the butter into the dry ingredients with your fingers or a pastry cutter until it looks like coarse bits.
10. The crumble filling is put on top of the apples in the tart.
11. Bake for 30 to 35 minutes in an oven that has already been warm or until the crust is golden brown and the apples are soft.
12. Take the tart out of the oven and let it cool for a few minutes in the pan before moving it to a wire rack to finish cooling.

APRICOT AND ALMOND CLAFOUTIS:

INGREDIENTS:
- 1 cup fresh apricots, pitted and halved
- 1/2 cup all-purpose flour
- 1/4 cup almond flour
- 1/2 cup granulated sugar
- Pinch of salt
- 3 large eggs
- 1 cup milk
- 1 teaspoon vanilla extract
- Powdered sugar (for dusting)

INSTRUCTIONS:
1. Set your oven to 375°F (190°C) and grease a baking dish or individual ramekins.
2. Set the apricot halves in a single layer in the baking dish or ramekins that have been greased.
3. Mix the all-purpose flour, almond flour, white sugar, and salt in a bowl with a whisk.
4. Whisk the eggs, milk, and vanilla extract in a separate bowl.
5. Gradually add the liquid and dry ingredients until smooth and well mixed.
6. Pour the batter on the apricots in the baking dish or ramekins.
7. Bake the clafoutis in an oven that has already been warm for 25 to 30 minutes or until the top is set and golden brown.
8. Take the clafoutis out of the oven and let it cool down for a few minutes.
9. Before you serve the Apricot and Almond Clafoutis, dust it with powdered sugar.

FRENCH ROASTED FIG TART:

INGREDIENTS:

For the Tart Crust:
- 1 1/4 cups all-purpose flour
- 1/4 cup granulated sugar
- 1/4 teaspoon salt
- 1/2 cup unsalted butter, cold and cut into small pieces
- 1 large egg yolk
- 1 tablespoon ice water

For the Fig Filling:
- 12-15 fresh figs, halved
- 1/4 cup honey
- 1 tablespoon lemon juice
- 1 teaspoon vanilla extract
- 1/2 teaspoon ground cinnamon

INSTRUCTIONS:

1. Set your oven to 375°F (190°C) and grease a tart pan.
2. Mix the all-purpose flour, sugar, and salt in a food processor. Mix by pulsing a few times.
3. Add the cold butter to the food processor and pulse until the mixture resembles coarse bits.
4. Whisk the egg yolk and ice water together in a small bowl. Add this to the food processor and pulse until the dough comes together.
5. Move the dough to a lightly floured surface and shape it into a ball. Cover with plastic wrap and put in the fridge for at least 30 minutes.
6. Roll out the cold dough into a circle big enough to fit your tart pan on a lightly floured surface. Press the dough into a tart pan that has been greased, and cut off any extra dough.
7. Mix the honey, lemon juice, vanilla extract, and ground cinnamon in a bowl with the figs cut in half.
8. Put an even layer of figs on top of the tart crust.
9. Pour any of the honey mixture that is left over on top of the figs.

10. Bake for 25 to 30 minutes in an oven that has already been warm or until the crust is golden brown and the figs are soft.
11. Take the tart out of the oven and let it cool for a few minutes in the pan before moving it to a wire rack to finish cooling.

BLUEBERRY LAVENDER POUND CAKE:

INGREDIENTS:

For the Pound Cake:
- 2 1/2 cups all-purpose flour
- 1 teaspoon baking powder
- 1/2 teaspoon salt
- 1 cup unsalted butter, softened
- 1 1/2 cups granulated sugar
- 4 large eggs
- 1 teaspoon vanilla extract
- 1/2 teaspoon dried culinary lavender
- 1 cup fresh blueberries

For the Glaze:
- 1 cup powdered sugar
- 1-2 tablespoons milk
- 1/2 teaspoon dried culinary lavender (optional)

INSTRUCTIONS:

1. Heat your oven to 350°F (175°C) and grease a loaf pan.
2. Mix the all-purpose flour, baking powder, and salt in a bowl with a whisk.
3. In a separate big bowl, beat the softened butter and granulated sugar until light and fluffy.
4. Add the eggs one by one and mix well after each one. Add the vanilla powder and lavender that has been dried.
5. Mix the dry ingredients slowly while stirring the butter mixture until a smooth batter forms.
6. Gently add the fresh blueberries.
7. Pour the batter into the pan that has been oiled, and use a spatula to smooth the top.

8. Bake in an oven that has been warm for 50 to 60 minutes or until a toothpick stuck in the middle comes out clean.
9. Take the pound cake out of the oven and let it cool for a few minutes in the pan before moving it to a wire rack to finish cooling.
10. Make the glaze by whisking the powdered sugar and milk in a small bowl. If wanted, stir in the dried lavender.
11. Pour the sauce over the pound cake once it has cooled.
12. Cut the Blueberry Lavender Pound Cake into pieces and serve it.

CHAPTER:7
VERRINES

CHOCOLATE MOUSSE VERRINE:

INGREDIENTS:
- 4 ounces dark chocolate, chopped
- 3/4 cup heavy cream
- 2 large egg yolks
- 2 tablespoons granulated sugar
- 1/2 teaspoon vanilla extract
- Whipped cream and chocolate shavings (for garnish)

INSTRUCTIONS:
1. Put the chopped dark chocolate in a bowl that can take the heat.
2. Heat the heavy cream in a small pot over medium heat until it simmer. Take it off the heat and pour it over the pieces of chocolate.
3. Let the mixture sit for a minute, then stir until the chocolate is fully melted and smooth. Put aside to cool down a bit.
4. Whisk the egg whites, sugar, and vanilla extract in a separate bowl until they are well mixed.
5. Pour the chocolate mixture slowly into the egg yolk mixture while mixing all the time.
6. Give each person an equal amount of chocolate mousse in a small glass or verrine.
7. Put in the fridge for at least two hours or until firm.
8. Before serving them, put whipped cream on top of the chocolate mousse verrines and sprinkle chocolate bits.

RASPBERRY AND LEMON CURD VERRINE:

INGREDIENTS:

- 1 cup fresh raspberries
- 1/2 cup lemon curd
- 1 cup whipped cream
- Lemon zest (for garnish)

INSTRUCTIONS:

1. Distribute the fresh raspberries evenly among the cups or verrines you use.
2. Spread lemon sauce on top of the raspberries.
3. Put some whipped cream on top.
4. Keep layering the ingredients until the verrines are full.
5. Add lemon zest to the top.
6. Refrigerate for at least 1 hour before serving.

STRAWBERRY TIRAMISU VERRINE:

INGREDIENTS:

- 1 cup strawberries, sliced
- 1 cup brewed coffee, cooled
- 1/2 cup mascarpone cheese
- 1/2 cup heavy cream
- 2 tablespoons powdered sugar
- 1/2 teaspoon vanilla extract
- Ladyfinger cookies
- Cocoa powder (for dusting)

INSTRUCTIONS:

1. Dip the ladyfinger cookies in the coffee, then dip a layer of cookies at the bottom of each serving glass or verrine.
2. Mix the mascarpone cheese, heavy cream, powdered sugar, and vanilla extract together in a bowl. Beat until thick and smooth.

3. Spread a layer of the mascarpone mixture on top of the ladyfingers that have been soaked.
4. Put sliced strawberries on top.
5. Repeat the steps until the verrines are full, ending with a layer of the mascarpone mixture.
6. The cocoa powder goes on top.
7. Refrigerate for at least 2 hours before serving.

PANNA COTTA AND MANGO VERRINE:

INGREDIENTS:

- 1 cup mango puree
- 1 1/2 cups heavy cream
- 1/4 cup granulated sugar
- 1 teaspoon vanilla extract
- 1 packet of unflavored gelatin
- Fresh mango chunks (for garnish)

INSTRUCTIONS:

1. Warm the mango puree in a small pot over low heat until it is warm. Set aside.
2. Mix the heavy cream, granulated sugar, and vanilla extract in a different pot. Bring to a simmer over medium heat.
3. Put the gelatin on top of 2 tablespoons of cold water in a small bowl and let it grow for a few minutes.
4. Take the cream mixture off the heat and stir until it is dissolved in the gelatin.
5. Add the warm mango juice and stir until everything is well-mixed.
6. Spread the mixture out evenly in each of the glasses or verrines.
7. Put in the fridge for at least four hours or until set.
8. Add chunks of fresh mango before serving.

CHOCOLATE AND SALTED CARAMEL VERRINE:

INGREDIENTS:

- 4 ounces dark chocolate, chopped
- 1 cup heavy cream
- 1/4 cup salted caramel sauce
- Whipped cream and chocolate shavings (for garnish)

INSTRUCTIONS:

1. Put the chopped dark chocolate in a bowl that can take the heat.
2. Heat the heavy cream in a small pot over medium heat until it starts to simmer. Take it off the heat and pour it over the pieces of chocolate.
3. Let the mixture sit for a minute, then stir it until the chocolate is fully melted and smooth. Put aside to cool down a bit.
4. Give each person an equal amount of chocolate mousse in a small glass or verrine.
5. Salt the caramel sauce and drizzle it over the chocolate mousse.
6. Add whipped cream and chocolate bits to the top.
7. Refrigerate for at least 2 hours before serving.

PEACH MELBA VERRINE:

INGREDIENTS:

- 1 cup fresh peaches, sliced
- 1/2 cup raspberry sauce or coulis
- 1 cup whipped cream
- Fresh raspberries (for garnish)

INSTRUCTIONS:

1. Spread the fresh peaches out evenly on each of the plates or verrines.
2. Spread raspberry sauce or coulis over the peaches with a spoon.
3. Put some whipped cream on top.
4. Keep layering the ingredients until the verrines are full.
5. Add fresh strawberries to the top.
6. Refrigerate for at least 1 hour before serving.

COCONUT AND PINEAPPLE VERRINE:

INGREDIENTS:
- 1 cup pineapple chunks
- 1 cup coconut cream
- 1/2 cup sweetened shredded coconut
- Whipped cream and toasted coconut flakes (for garnish)

INSTRUCTIONS:
1. Divide the pineapple chunks between the serving glasses or verrines in an even way.
2. Spread coconut cream on top of the pineapple.
3. Spread a layer of sweetened coconut shreds.
4. Keep layering the ingredients until the verrines are full.
5. Toast coconut flakes and put them on top of whipped cream.
6. Refrigerate for at least 1 hour before serving.

ESPRESSO AND CHOCOLATE VERRINE:

INGREDIENTS:
- 1 cup espresso or strong brewed coffee, cooled
- 1/2 cup mascarpone cheese
- 1/2 cup heavy cream
- 2 tablespoons powdered sugar
- 1/2 teaspoon vanilla extract
- Chocolate shavings (for garnish)

INSTRUCTIONS:

1. Put a layer of ladyfinger cookies that have been dipped in espresso or brewed coffee at the bottom of each serving glass or verrine.
2. Mix the mascarpone cheese, heavy cream, powdered sugar, and vanilla extract together in a bowl. Beat until thick and smooth.
3. Spread a layer of the mascarpone mixture on top of the ladyfingers that have been soaked.
4. Repeat the steps until the verrines are full, ending with a layer of the mascarpone mixture.
5. Sprinkle chocolate pieces on top.
6. Refrigerate for at least 2 hours before serving.

CHERRY AND VANILLA CREAM VERRINE:

INGREDIENTS:

- 1 cup cherries, pitted and halved
- 1 cup vanilla pastry cream
- 1 cup whipped cream
- Fresh mint leaves (for garnish)

INSTRUCTIONS:

1. Put an equal amount of cherries in each serving glass or verrine.
2. Spread some vanilla pastry cream on top of the cherries.
3. Put some whipped cream on top.
4. Keep layering the ingredients until the verrines are full.
5. Add some fresh mint leaves to the top.
6. Refrigerate for at least 1 hour before serving.

LEMON MERINGUE VERRINE:

INGREDIENTS:
- 1 cup lemon curd
- 1 cup whipped cream
- Crushed graham crackers (for garnish)
- Lemon zest (for garnish)
- Mini meringue cookies (for garnish)

INSTRUCTIONS:
1. Spread the lemon curd out evenly in each of the cups or verrines.
2. Spread whipped cream on top of the lemon curd.
3. Crush some graham crackers and sprinkle them on top.
4. Add lemon juice and small meringue cookies to the top.
5. Refrigerate for at least 1 hour before serving.

RASPBERRY AND PISTACHIO VERRINE:

INGREDIENTS:
- 1 cup fresh raspberries
- 1/2 cup pistachio pastry cream
- 1 cup whipped cream
- Crushed pistachios (for garnish)

INSTRUCTIONS:
1. Distribute the fresh raspberries evenly among the cups or verrines you use.
2. Spread pistachio pastry cream over the strawberries in a layer.
3. Put some whipped cream on top.
4. Keep layering the ingredients until the verrines are full.
5. Sprinkle crushed nuts on top.
6. Refrigerate for at least 1 hour before serving.

CHOCOLATE AND RASPBERRY VERRINE:

INGREDIENTS:

- 4 ounces dark chocolate, chopped
- 1 cup heavy cream
- 1 cup fresh raspberries
- Whipped cream and chocolate shavings (for garnish)

INSTRUCTIONS:

1. Put the chopped dark chocolate in a bowl that can take the heat.
2. Heat the heavy cream in a small pot over medium heat until it simmer. Take it off the heat and pour it over the pieces of chocolate.
3. Let the mixture sit for a minute, then stir until the chocolate is fully melted and smooth. Put aside to cool down a bit.
4. Give each person an equal amount of chocolate mousse in a small glass or verrine.
5. Add fresh strawberries to the top.
6. Add whipped cream and chocolate bits to the top.
7. Refrigerate for at least 2 hours before serving.

TIRAMISU AND BERRY VERRINE:

INGREDIENTS:

- 1 cup tiramisu filling or mascarpone cheese
- 1 cup mixed berries (such as strawberries, raspberries, and blueberries)
- Ladyfinger cookies, crushed
- Cocoa powder (for dusting)

INSTRUCTIONS:

1. Divide the tiramisu filling or mascarpone cheese evenly between the glasses or verrines you will use to serve the dessert.
2. On top of the sauce, add a layer of mixed berries.

3. Crushed ladyfinger cookies should be sprinkled on top.
4. Use chocolate powder to dust.
5. Keep layering the ingredients until the verrines are full.
6. Refrigerate for at least 1 hour before serving.

MINT CHOCOLATE MOUSSE VERRINE:

INGREDIENTS:
- 4 ounces dark chocolate, chopped
- 1 cup heavy cream
- 1/2 teaspoon peppermint extract
- Green food coloring (optional)
- Whipped cream and chocolate shavings (for garnish)

INSTRUCTIONS:
1. Put the chopped dark chocolate in a bowl that can take the heat.
2. Heat the heavy cream in a small pot over medium heat until it simmer. Take it off the heat and pour it over the pieces of chocolate.
3. Let the mixture sit for a minute, then stir until the chocolate is fully melted and smooth. Put aside to cool down a bit.
4. Add the peppermint flavor and the green food coloring to the chocolate mixture if you are using it. Stir until the mixture is smooth.
5. Spread the mint chocolate mousse evenly in small glasses or verrines for each person.
6. Add whipped cream and chocolate bits to the top.
7. Refrigerate for at least 2 hours before serving.

VANILLA CUSTARD AND STRAWBERRY VERRINE:

INGREDIENTS:

- 1 cup vanilla custard
- 1 cup fresh strawberries, sliced
- Crushed shortbread cookies (for garnish)
- Fresh mint leaves (for garnish)

INSTRUCTIONS:

1. Divide the vanilla custard fairly among the glasses or verrines you will use to serve it.
2. Strawberry slices go on top of the cream.
3. Crush some shortbread cookies and sprinkle them on top.
4. Add some fresh mint leaves to the top.
5. Refrigerate for at least 1 hour before serving.

CHAPTER:8
FROZEN OR REFRIGERATED DESSERTS

GLACÉ AU CHOCOLAT (CHOCOLATE ICE CREAM):

INGREDIENTS:
- 2 cups heavy cream
- 1 cup whole milk
- 3/4 cup granulated sugar
- 1/2 cup unsweetened cocoa powder
- 4 large egg yolks
- 1 teaspoon vanilla extract
- 4 ounces dark chocolate, chopped

INSTRUCTIONS:
1. Over medium heat, bring the heavy cream, whole milk, granulated sugar, and cocoa powder to a simmer in a pot. Take off the heat.
2. Whisk the egg whites in a separate bowl until they are smooth.
3. Pour a small amount of the hot cream mixture into the egg yolks slowly while mixing. This will warm up the yolks and keep them from scrambling.
4. Whisk the egg whites heated in the pan with the rest of the cream mixture.
5. Put the pan back on the stove over low heat and stir until it gets thick enough to coat the back of a spoon. Do not let it boil.
6. Take the pot off the heat and stir in the vanilla extract and chopped dark chocolate until the chocolate is melted and the mixture is smooth.

7. Let the mixture cool to room temperature, then cover and put it in the fridge for at least 4 hours or overnight.
8. Once the liquid has cooled, churn it in an ice cream maker according to the instructions that came with it.
9. Put the churned ice cream in a container with a lid and freeze it for at least two hours or until it is hard.
10. Glacé au Chocolat can be served in bowls or cones. Enjoy!

TARTE AU CITRON GELÉE (FROZEN LEMON TART):

INGREDIENTS:
For the Crust:
- 1 1/2 cups graham cracker crumbs
- 1/4 cup granulated sugar
- 1/2 cup unsalted butter, melted
For the Lemon Filling:
- 1 cup lemon juice
- 1 tablespoon lemon zest
- 1 cup granulated sugar
- 4 large eggs
- 1/2 cup unsalted butter, cubed
For the Gelée Topping:
- 1/2 cup water
- 1/4 cup granulated sugar
- 1 tablespoon lemon juice
- 1 teaspoon gelatin powder

INSTRUCTIONS:
1. Mix the graham cracker crumbs, sugar, and melted butter for the crust in a bowl. Mix until all of the pieces are covered.
2. Press the crumb mixture into the bottom and sides of a pie pan to cover it evenly. Put pressure on it with the back of a spoon or the bottom of a glass.
3. Put the crust in the freezer for 15 to 20 minutes to harden.

4. Mix the lemon juice, zest, sugar, and eggs in a pot for the lemon filling. Whisk until the mixture is smooth.
5. Put the pot on low heat and put the butter cubes in it. Keep stirring the mixture as it cooks until it gets thick enough to coat the back of a spoon.
6. Take the lemon filling off the heat and let it cool to room temperature.
7. Pour the lemon filling, left to cool, into the cold bread and spread it evenly.
8. For the gelée topping, mix the water, sugar, lemon juice, and gelatin powder in a small pot. Stir while heating on low heat until all the gelatin is dissolved.
9. Let the gelée mixture cool down, then pour it over the lemon filling in the tart.
10. Put the tart in the refrigerator for at least 4 hours or until the gelée has set.
11. Once the tart is set, remove it from the fridge and let it sit at room temperature for a few minutes before cutting it into pieces and serving it.

PARFAIT AUX FRUITS ROUGES (BERRY PARFAIT):

INGREDIENTS:
- 2 cups mixed fresh berries (such as strawberries, blueberries, raspberries)
- 1 cup heavy cream
- 1/4 cup powdered sugar
- 1 teaspoon vanilla extract
- 1 cup Greek yogurt
- Honey (optional)

INSTRUCTIONS:
1. Mix the fresh berries gently in a large bowl.
2. Heavy cream, powdered sugar, and vanilla extract are mixed in a separate bowl until stiff peaks form.

3. Mix the Greek yogurt and whipped cream until they are well mixed.
4. The fruit mixture goes on the bottom of parfait glasses or dessert cups. Then the whipped cream mixture goes on top.
5. Repeat the layers until the glasses are full, finishing with a dollop of the whipped cream mixture on top.
6. If you want, drizzle with honey.
7. Refrigerate for at least 1 hour before serving.

CAFÉ LIÉGEOIS (COFFEE AND ICE CREAM DESSERT):

INGREDIENTS:
- 1 cup strong brewed coffee, cooled
- 1 cup vanilla ice cream
- Whipped cream
- Chocolate shavings or cocoa powder (for garnish)

INSTRUCTIONS:
1. Pour the coffee into serving cups after it has had time to cool.
2. Give each glass a scoop of vanilla ice cream.
3. Add whipped cream on top.
4. Add chocolate bits or cocoa powder on top.
5. Serve the Café Liégeois right away and enjoy it.

FRENCH CHOCOLATE SEMIFREDDO:

INGREDIENTS:
- 4 ounces dark chocolate, chopped
- 3 large eggs separated
- 1/2 cup granulated sugar
- 1 teaspoon vanilla extract
- 1 cup heavy cream, whipped

INSTRUCTIONS:

1. Melt the chopped dark chocolate in a bowl that can handle heat set over a pot of boiling water. Mix until it's smooth. Take it off the heat and let it cool down a bit.
2. Whisk the egg whites, sugar, and vanilla extract together until they are well mixed.
3. Pour the melting chocolate into the egg yolk mixture slowly, whisking all the time to mix.
4. Beat the egg whites in a different bowl until stiff peaks form.
5. Fold the whipped egg whites into the chocolate mixture gently until everything is well mixed.
6. Put the whipped cream in.
7. Pour the semifreddo filling into a loaf pan or ramekins.
8. Wrap it in plastic wrap and put it in the freezer for at least 6 hours or until it is firm.
9. Before serving it, take it out of the freezer and let it sit at room temperature for a few minutes so it can soften a bit.
10. The French Chocolate Semifreddo can be served in slices or scoops.

SORBET À LA FRAMBOISE (RASPBERRY SORBET):

INGREDIENTS:
- 4 cups fresh or frozen raspberries
- 1 cup granulated sugar
- 1 cup water
- 1 tablespoon lemon juice

INSTRUCTIONS:
1. Mix the strawberries, sugar, water, and lemon juice together in a saucepan.
2. Over medium heat, stir the mixture occasionally as it comes to a boil.
3. Cook for about 5 minutes, until the raspberries have broken down and the sugar has melted.
4. Take the mix off the heat and let it cool to room temperature.

5. Pour the liquid into a blender or food processor and blend it until it is smooth.
6. Use a fine-mesh sieve to remove any seeds from the mixture.
7. Pour the mixture separated into an ice cream maker and churn it as directed by the manufacturer.
8. Put the sorbet in a jar with a lid and freeze it for at least four hours or until it is firm.
9. Sorbet à la Framboise can be served in bowls or cones. Enjoy!

MOCHA POTS DE CRÈME:

INGREDIENTS:
- 1 cup heavy cream
- 1/2 cup whole milk
- 2 tablespoons instant coffee granules
- 4 ounces dark chocolate, chopped
- 4 large egg yolks
- 1/4 cup granulated sugar
- 1 teaspoon vanilla extract
- Whipped cream and chocolate shavings (for garnish)

INSTRUCTIONS:
1. Over medium heat, bring the heavy cream, whole milk, and instant coffee granules to a simmer in a pot. Take off the heat.
2. Put the pieces of dark chocolate in the pan and let it sit for a minute to melt. Mix until it's smooth.
3. Whisk the egg whites, sugar, and vanilla extract in a separate bowl until they are well mixed.
4. Slowly pour a small amount of chocolate into the egg yolk mixture while mixing constantly to temper the egg yolks.
5. Whisk the egg whites heated in the pan with the rest of the chocolate mixture.
6. Pour the mix through a sieve with a fine mesh to eliminate lumps.
7. Put the same amount of the mixture into each pot de crème cup or dish.

8. Put the cups or ramekins in a baking dish and fill the dish with hot water until it comes about halfway up the sides of the cups.
9. Carefully place the baking dish in a preheated oven and bake at 325°F (160°C) for about 30 minutes, or until the sides are set, but the centers are still slightly jiggly.
10. Take the pots de crème out of the water bath and let them cool down until they are at room temperature.
11. Put in the fridge for at least two hours or until it's cold and firm.
12. Before you serve, put whipped cream on top of each pot de crème and sprinkle chocolate bits.

FLEUR DE LAIT (PHILADELPHIA-STYLE ICE CREAM):

INGREDIENTS:
- 2 cups heavy cream
- 1 cup whole milk
- 3/4 cup granulated sugar
- 2 teaspoons vanilla extract

INSTRUCTIONS:
1. Whisk the heavy cream, whole milk, powdered sugar, and vanilla extract together until the sugar is gone.
2. Pour the liquid into an ice cream maker and follow the directions on the machine.
3. Once the ice cream has been churned, put it in a jar with a lid and freeze it for at least 4 hours or until it is firm.
4. Fleur de Lait can be served in bowls or cones.

CHOCOLATE CHERRY ICE CREAM BOMBE:

INGREDIENTS:

- 2 pints of cherry ice cream
- 1 pint chocolate ice cream
- 1 cup chocolate cookie crumbs
- 1/2 cup chopped cherries
- Chocolate sauce and whipped cream (for garnish)

INSTRUCTIONS:

1. Line a mixing bowl or bombe mold that holds 2 quarts with plastic wrap, leaving enough extra to cover the top.
2. The cherry ice cream and chocolate ice cream will be easier to work with if you soften them a bit.
3. Spread the softened cherry ice cream evenly on the bottom of the bowl lined with a paper towel.
4. On top of the cherry ice cream layer, sprinkle half of the chocolate cookie crumbs and half of the chopped cherries.
5. Spread out the chocolate ice cream that has been warmed and put it on top of the cherry ice cream layer.
6. On top of the chocolate ice cream, sprinkle the rest of the chocolate cookie pieces and the chopped cherries.
7. Fold the plastic wrap that hangs over the top of the ice cream bombe to cover it completely.
8. Put the bombe in the freezer and let it stay there for at least four hours or until it is firm.
9. Carefully remove the bombe from the mold and place it on a serving board. Remove the plastic wrap.
10. Pour chocolate sauce over the Chocolate Cherry Ice Cream Bombe and top with whipped cream.
11. Cut and serve right away.

VANILLA AND PRALINE BÛCHE DE NOËL ICE CREAM CAKE:

INGREDIENTS:
- 1-quart vanilla ice cream
- 1/2 cup praline paste or crushed praline candies
- 1/2 cup chopped toasted hazelnuts or almonds
- 8 ounces chocolate ganache
- Whipped cream and chocolate shavings (for garnish)

INSTRUCTIONS:
1. Line a Bûche de Nol pan or a loaf pan with plastic wrap, leaving enough overflow to cover the top.
2. To make it easier to work with, soften the vanilla ice cream.
3. Spread a layer of vanilla ice cream that has been warmed and smoothed out on the bottom of the pan or mold that has been lined.
4. On top of the vanilla ice cream layer, sprinkle half of the praline paste or crushed praline candies and half of the chopped toasted hazelnuts or almonds.
5. Spread another layer of vanilla ice cream warmed and smoothed out on top.
6. On top of the second layer of vanilla ice cream, sprinkle the rest of the praline paste, crushed praline candies, and the chopped toasted hazelnuts or almonds.
7. Fold the plastic wrap hanging over the ice cream cake's top to cover it completely.
8. Put the cake in the freezer for at least four hours or until it is hard.
9. Carefully take the cake from the pan and place it on a serving plate. Remove the plastic wrap.
10. Pour the chocolate ganache over the top of the cake and let it run down the sides.
11. Put whipped cream on top and put chocolate shavings on top.
12. Cut and serve the Vanilla and Praline Bûche de Nol Ice Cream Cake into pieces.

STRAWBERRY CHAMPAGNE SORBET:

INGREDIENTS:

- 2 cups fresh or frozen strawberries
- 1/2 cup granulated sugar
- 1 cup champagne or sparkling wine
- 1 tablespoon lemon juice

INSTRUCTIONS:

1. Blend or process the strawberries, sugar, champagne, and lemon juice in a mixer or food processor.
2. Mix until it's smooth.
3. Pour the mix through a sieve with a fine mesh to remove any seeds.
4. Pour the mixture separated into an ice cream maker and churn it as directed by the manufacturer.
5. Put the sorbet in a jar with a lid and freeze it for at least four hours or until it is firm.
6. Strawberry Champagne Sorbet can be served in bowls or cones. Enjoy!

FRENCH SILK PIE ICE CREAM:

INGREDIENTS:

- 2 cups heavy cream
- 1 cup whole milk
- 3/4 cup granulated sugar
- 3 tablespoons unsweetened cocoa powder
- 4 ounces dark chocolate, chopped
- 4 large eggs
- 1 teaspoon vanilla extract
- Chocolate cookie crumbs (optional for garnish)

INSTRUCTIONS:

1. Over medium heat, bring the heavy cream, whole milk, granulated sugar, and cocoa powder to a simmer in a pot. Take off the heat.
2. Put the pieces of dark chocolate in the pan and let it sit for a minute to melt. Mix until it's smooth.
3. Whisk the eggs and vanilla extract together in a different bowl until they are well mixed.
4. To temper the eggs, slowly pour a small amount of chocolate into the egg mixture while stirring.
5. Whisk the tempered egg mixture into the pot's rest of the chocolate mixture.
6. Pour the mix through a sieve with a fine mesh to get rid of any lumps.
7. Put the pan back on the stove over low heat and stir the mixture constantly until it gets thick enough to coat the back of a spoon.
8. Take the mix off the heat and let it cool to room temperature.
9. Cover and put in the fridge for at least 4 hours or overnight.
10. Once the liquid has cooled, pour it into an ice cream maker and use it as directed by the maker.
11. Put the churned ice cream in a container with a lid and freeze it for at least two hours or until it is hard.
12. Serve the French Silk Pie ice cream in bowls or cones; if you want, top it with bits of chocolate cookie.

CHOCOLATE LAVENDER SORBET:

INGREDIENTS:

- 2 cups water
- 1 cup granulated sugar
- 1/2 cup unsweetened cocoa powder
- 2 tablespoons dried lavender flowers
- 1 tablespoon lemon juice

INSTRUCTIONS:

1. Mix the water, sugar, cocoa powder, and dried lavender flowers together in a pot.
2. Over medium heat, bring the mixture to a boil, stirring to melt the sugar and cocoa powder.
3. Take it off the heat and let it sit for about 10 minutes.
4. Use a fine-mesh sieve to remove the lavender flowers from the mixture.
5. Add the lemon juice and stir.
6. Let the mixture cool to room temperature, then cover and put it in the fridge for at least 4 hours or overnight.
7. Once the liquid has cooled, pour it into an ice cream maker and use it as directed by the maker.
8. Put the sorbet in a jar with a lid and freeze it for at least four hours or until it is firm.
9. Chocolate lavender sorbet can be served in bowls or cones. Enjoy!

POIRE BELLE HÉLÈNE (POACHED PEARS WITH CHOCOLATE SAUCE AND ICE CREAM):

INGREDIENTS:
- 4 ripe but firm pears
- 1 cup red wine
- 1/2 cup granulated sugar
- 1 cinnamon stick
- 4 scoops vanilla ice cream
- Chocolate sauce
- Slivered almonds (for garnish)

INSTRUCTIONS:
1. Mix the red wine, sugar, and cinnamon sticks together in a pot.
2. Over medium heat, bring the mixture to a boil and stir to melt the sugar.
3. Turn down the heat and put in the pears. Simmer for about 20 minutes or until the pears are soft but still have their shape.
4. Take the pears out of the liquid used to cook them and let them cool.
5. When the pears are cool, cut them in half lengthwise and take out the core.
6. Put a scoop of vanilla ice cream on a bowl or plate.
7. Place a half of a pear that has been cooked next to the ice cream.
8. Pour chocolate sauce over the ice cream and pears.
9. Spread sliced almonds on top.
10. Do the same thing with the rest of the pears.
11. Use a spoon to serve the Poire Belle Hélène and enjoy!

NOUGAT GLACÉ (FROZEN NOUGAT):

INGREDIENTS:
- 1 1/2 cups heavy cream
- 1/2 cup honey
- 4 large egg whites
- 1/2 cup chopped mixed nuts (such as almonds, pistachios, and hazelnuts)
- 1/4 cup chopped dried fruits (such as apricots, cranberries, and cherries)
- 1/4 cup mini chocolate chips

INSTRUCTIONS:
1. Whip the heavy cream in a bowl until soft peaks form.
2. Heat the honey in a different bowl in the microwave or on the stove until it is warm.
3. While the honey is getting warm, beat the egg whites in a clean bowl until they make stiff peaks.
4. Slowly pour the warm honey into the egg whites that have been beaten, mixing all the time to mix it in.
5. Mix the whipped cream gently with the egg white and honey.
6. Mix in the small chocolate chips, chopped nuts, and dried fruit.
7. Pour the batter into a loaf pan or into ramekins for each person.
8. Wrap it in plastic wrap and put it in the freezer for at least 6 hours or until it is firm.
9. Before serving the nougat glacé, take it out of the freezer and let it sit at room temperature for a few minutes to soften a bit.
10. The Nougat Glacé can be cut or scooped out and served.

CARAMEL AND PECAN ICE CREAM TERRINE:

INGREDIENTS:
- 2 pints caramel ice cream
- 1/2 cup chopped toasted pecans
- Caramel sauce
- Whipped cream (for garnish)

INSTRUCTIONS:
1. Line a loaf pan with plastic wrap, leaving enough extra to cover the top.
2. The caramel ice cream will be easier to work with if you soften it a little.
3. Spread a layer of caramel ice cream that has been warmed in the bottom of the loaf pan.
4. Put half of the chopped, toasted nuts on top of the ice cream.
5. Repeat with more caramel ice cream and the rest of the nuts.
6. Fold the plastic wrap hanging over the ice cream terrine's top to cover it completely.
7. Put the terrine in the freezer and let it stay there for at least 4 hours or until it is solid.
8. Before serving, carefully take the terrine from the mold and place it on a serving platter.
9. Sprinkle with whipped cream and drizzle with caramel sauce.
10. Cut the Caramel and Pecan Ice Cream Terrine into pieces and serve it.

CITRON ET BASILIC SORBET (LEMON BASIL SORBET):

INGREDIENTS:

- 2 cups water
- 1 cup granulated sugar
- 1 cup fresh lemon juice
- 2 tablespoons lemon zest
- 1/4 cup fresh basil leaves, chopped

INSTRUCTIONS:

1. Put the water and powdered sugar in a saucepan.
2. Over medium heat, bring the mixture to a boil and stir to melt the sugar.
3. Take the syrup off the heat and let it cool to room temperature.
4. Mix in the fresh lemon juice, lemon zest, and fresh basil that has been chopped.
5. Pour the liquid into an ice cream maker and follow the directions on the machine.
6. Put the sorbet in a jar with a lid and freeze it for at least four hours or until it is firm.
7. The Citron et Basilic Sorbet can be served in bowls or cones.

ESPRESSO GRANITA:

INGREDIENTS:

- 2 cups strong brewed espresso or coffee
- 1/2 cup granulated sugar
- Whipped cream (for garnish)

INSTRUCTIONS:

1. In a saucepan, mix the sugar with the espresso or coffee that has been made.

2. Stir while heating over medium heat until the sugar is completely dissolved.
3. Take the mix off the heat and let it cool to room temperature.
4. Pour the mixture into a small dish that can go in the freezer.
5. Put the dish in the freezer and let it stay there for an hour.
6. After an hour, scrape the half-frozen liquid with a fork to break up any ice crystals.
7. Put the dish back in the freezer and let it stay there for an hour.
8. Repeat the scraping process every hour for 4 to 6 hours or until the granita has a slushy structure.
9. Serve the Espresso Granita in cups or bowls with whipped cream on top.

RASPBERRY AND ROSEMARY GELATO:

INGREDIENTS:
- 2 cups fresh or frozen raspberries
- 1 cup whole milk
- 1 cup heavy cream
- 3/4 cup granulated sugar
- 2 sprigs fresh rosemary
- 4 large egg yolks

INSTRUCTIONS:
1. Puree the raspberries in a mixer or food processor until they are smooth. Use a fine-mesh sieve to remove the seeds from the puree. Set aside.
2. Mix the milk, heavy cream, sugar, and rosemary leaves together in a saucepan. Warm up the mixture over medium heat until it starts to simmer. Take the rosemary off the heat and let it sit for about 10 minutes.
3. Whisk the egg whites in a separate bowl until they are smooth.
4. Pour a little bit of the hot milk mixture into the egg yolks at a time while mixing. This will temper the egg yolks.

5. Whisk the egg whites slowly into the pan with the rest of the milk mixture.
6. Put the pan back on the stove over low heat and stir the mixture constantly until it gets thick enough to coat the back of a spoon.
7. Take the mixture off the heat and pour it through a fine-mesh sieve to get rid of the rosemary leaves.
8. Add the raspberry sauce and stir until everything is well-mixed.
9. Let the mixture cool to room temperature, then cover and put it in the fridge for at least 4 hours or overnight.
10. Once the liquid has cooled, pour it into an ice cream maker and use it as directed by the maker.
11. Put the churned gelato in a jar with a lid and freeze it for at least 2 hours or until it is firm.
12. The Raspberry and Rosemary Gelato can be served in bowls or cones.

CHOCOLATE MINT SEMIFREDDO

INGREDIENTS:
- 8 ounces dark chocolate, chopped
- 1 cup heavy cream
- 1/2 cup fresh mint leaves
- 4 large egg yolks
- 1/4 cup granulated sugar
- 1 teaspoon vanilla extract
- 1/4 teaspoon peppermint extract
- Whipped cream and chocolate shavings for garnish (optional)

INSTRUCTIONS:
1. Melt the dark chocolate in a bowl that can handle heat over a pot of water that is just about to boil. Mix until it's smooth. Take it off the heat and let it cool down a bit.

2. Heat the heavy cream in a small pot until it starts to bubble. Take off the heat.
3. Add the fresh mint leaves to the hot cream and sit for about 10 minutes.
4. To get rid of the mint leaves, strain the cream and press down on the leaves to get as much flavor as possible.
5. Whisk the egg whites, sugar, vanilla extract, and peppermint extract together until everything is well mixed.
6. Put the bowl over a pan of boiling water and whisk the mixture constantly for about 5 to 7 minutes or until it thickens and has custard consistency.
7. Take the bowl off the stove and whisk it for another minute to cool it down.
8. Pour the melting chocolate in small amounts into the custard mixture while whisking constantly.
9. Whip the heavy cream in a different bowl until soft peaks form.
10. Mix the whipped cream gently into the chocolate custard mixture until everything is well mixed.
11. Pour the batter into a loaf pan or into ramekins for each person.
12. Wrap it in plastic wrap and put it in the freezer for at least 6 hours or until it is firm.
13. Before serving it, take it out of the freezer and let it sit at room temperature for a few minutes so it can soften a bit.
14. If you want, you can decorate with whipped cream and chocolate bits.
15. Cut the Chocolate Mint Semifreddo into slices or scoops and serve.

CHAPTER:9
WAFFLES, CREPES, AND PANCAKES

CRÊPES SUZETTE:

INGREDIENTS:
- 1 cup all-purpose flour
- 2 tablespoons granulated sugar
- 1/4 teaspoon salt
- 3 large eggs
- 1 cup milk
- 1/4 cup orange liqueur (such as Grand Marnier)
- 2 tablespoons unsalted butter, melted
- Zest of 1 orange
- Juice of 1 orange
- 2 tablespoons unsalted butter
- 2 tablespoons granulated sugar
- 2 tablespoons orange liqueur (such as Grand Marnier)

INSTRUCTIONS:
1. Whisk the flour, sugar, and salt together in a bowl.
2. In a different bowl, beat the eggs and milk together until they are well mixed.
3. Pour the egg and milk mixture into the flour mixture slowly while whisking. Keep whisking until you have a smooth batter.
4. Mix in the orange liquor, orange zest, and melted butter.
5. Heat a skillet or crêpe pan that doesn't stick over medium heat.
6. Use a little butter or cooking spray to grease the pan.
7. Pour about 1/4 cup of batter into the middle of the pan. Tilt and swirl the pan to spread the batter evenly into a thin circle.

8. Cook the crêpe for about one to two minutes, or until the sides start to lift and the bottom is golden brown.
9. Turn the crêpe over and cook for another 1–2 minutes.
10. Repeat with the rest of the dough, greasing the pan as necessary.
11. Melt the butter in a different pot over medium heat.
12. Add the sugar and orange juice and stir until the sugar is melted.
13. Add the orange liqueur, stir, and cook for another minute.
14. Take the pan off the heat.
15. Each crêpe should be folded in half, then in half again to make a triangle.
16. Fold the crêpes in half and put them in the pan with the orange sauce. Turn the crêpes to cover them with the sauce.
17. Put the pan back on low heat for another minute to let the crêpes soak up the sauce.
18. You can top the warm Crêpes Suzette with orange zest or vanilla ice cream and drizzle them with more sauce.

GAUFRES DE LIÈGE (LIEGE WAFFLES):

INGREDIENTS:
- 2 1/4 cups all-purpose flour
- 1/2 cup pearl sugar
- 1/2 cup unsalted butter, melted
- 3/4 cup warm milk
- 2 large eggs
- 2 teaspoons active dry yeast
- 1 teaspoon vanilla extract
- Pinch of salt

INSTRUCTIONS:
1. Dissolve the yeast in the warm milk in a small bowl and let it sit for about 5 minutes or until it becomes foamy.
2. Mix the flour and salt in a big bowl.

3.   Make a well in the middle of the flour mixture and pour in the yeast mixture, melted butter, eggs, and vanilla extract.
4.   Mix the ingredients until you have a sticky dough.
5.   Cover the bowl with a clean cooking towel and put it somewhere warm for about an hour or until the dough has doubled.
6.   Fold the pearl sugar into the dough gently until it is spread out evenly.
7.   Follow the directions on the box to heat a waffle iron.
8.   Use a little butter or cooking spray to grease the waffle pan.
9.   Spoon some of the dough into the middle of the waffle iron, which has already been heated, and spread it out slightly to cover the area.
10. Close the waffle press and cook for about 3 to 5 minutes or until the waffle is golden brown and crisp.
11. Carefully take the waffle out of the iron and cook the rest of the dough the same way.
12. Serve the Gaufres de Liège warm, with or without toppings like powdered sugar, whipped cream, or fresh berries.

CRÊPES AU CHOCOLAT (CHOCOLATE CREPES):

INGREDIENTS:
- 1 cup all-purpose flour
- 2 tablespoons unsweetened cocoa powder
- 2 tablespoons granulated sugar
- 1/4 teaspoon salt
- 3 large eggs
- 1 cup milk
- 1/2 cup water
- 2 tablespoons unsalted butter, melted
- Chocolate hazelnut spread (such as Nutella) for filling
- Fresh berries and powdered sugar for garnish

INSTRUCTIONS:

1. Whisk the flour, chocolate powder, sugar, and salt in a bowl.
2. Mix the eggs, milk, water, and melted butter in a different bowl with a whisk until everything is well mixed.
3. Pour the egg and milk mixture into the flour mixture slowly while whisking. Keep whisking until you have a smooth batter.
4. Heat a skillet or crêpe pan that doesn't stick over medium heat.
5. Use a little butter or cooking spray to grease the pan.
6. Pour about 1/4 cup of batter into the middle of the pan. Tilt and swirl the pan to spread the batter evenly into a thin circle.
7. Cook the crêpe for about one to two minutes or until the sides lift and the bottom is set.
8. Turn the crêpe over and cook for another 1–2 minutes.
9. Repeat with the rest of the dough, greasing the pan as necessary.
10. On one half of each crêpe, spread a thin layer of chocolate hazelnut spread.
11. Fold the crêpe in half, then in half again to make a triangle.
12. Serve the Crêpes au Chocolat hot, with powdered sugar on top and fresh berries on the side.

BUCKWHEAT GALETTES WITH HAM AND CHEESE:

INGREDIENTS:
- 1 cup buckwheat flour
- 1/2 cup all-purpose flour
- 1/2 teaspoon salt
- 2 large eggs
- 2 cups water
- 4 slices of ham
- 1 cup grated Gruyère or Emmental cheese
- Salted butter for cooking

INSTRUCTIONS:

1. Mix the buckwheat, all-purpose, and salt in a bowl with a whisk.
2. In a different bowl, beat the eggs and slowly add the water while whisking until everything is well mixed.
3. Pour the egg and water mixture into the flour mixture slowly while whisking. Keep whisking until you have a smooth batter.
4. Let the batter sit for at least 30 minutes so the buckwheat flour can soak up water.
5. Heat a skillet or crêpe pan that doesn't stick over medium heat.
6. Add salted butter to the pan and move it around to cover the surface.
7. Pour about 1/4 cup of batter into the middle of the pan. Tilt and swirl the pan to spread the batter evenly into a thin circle.
8. Cook the galette for about 2 to 3 minutes, or until the edges pull away from the pan and the bottom is golden brown.
9. Turn the galette over and cook on the other side for 2–3 minutes.
10. Take the galette out of the pan and put it somewhere warm.
11. Repeat with the rest of the batter. If you need to, add more butter to the pan.
12. Put a piece of ham and some grated cheese on one half of ·each galette.
13. Fold the galette in half, then in half again to make a triangle.
14. Serve the Galettes with Ham and Cheese while they are still warm.

WAFFLES WITH LAVENDER HONEY AND BERRIES:

INGREDIENTS:

- 2 cups all-purpose flour
- 1/4 cup granulated sugar
- 1 tablespoon baking powder
- 1/2 teaspoon salt
- 2 large eggs
- 1 3/4 cups milk
- 1/2 cup unsalted butter, melted
- 1 teaspoon vanilla extract
- Lavender honey (or regular honey) for drizzling
- Fresh berries for topping

INSTRUCTIONS:

1. Whisk the flour, sugar, baking powder, and salt together in a bowl.
2. In a different bowl, whisk the eggs, milk, melted butter, vanilla extract, and salt together until everything is well mixed.
3. Pour the egg and milk mixture into the flour mixture slowly while whisking. Keep whisking until you have a smooth batter.
4. Follow the directions on the box to heat up a waffle iron.
5. Use a little butter or cooking spray to grease the waffle pan.
6. Spoon some batter into the center of the waffle iron, which has already been heated, and spread it out a bit to cover the area.
7. Close the waffle maker and let it cook until golden brown and crisp.
8. Repeat with the rest of the dough.
9. Serve the waffles with honey lavender and fresh berries on top.

CRÊPES WITH ORANGE AND GRAND MARNIER:

INGREDIENTS:
- 1 cup all-purpose flour
- 2 tablespoons granulated sugar
- 1/4 teaspoon salt
- 3 large eggs
- 1 cup milk
- 1/4 cup orange liqueur (such as Grand Marnier)
- 2 tablespoons unsalted butter, melted
- Zest of 1 orange
- Juice of 1 orange
- Powdered sugar for dusting

INSTRUCTIONS:
1. Whisk the flour, sugar, and salt together in a bowl.
2. In a different bowl, beat the eggs and milk together until they are well mixed.
3. Pour the egg and milk mixture into the flour mixture slowly while whisking. Keep whisking until you have a smooth batter.
4. Mix in the orange juice, peel, orange juice, and liqueur.
5. Heat a skillet or crêpe pan that doesn't stick over medium heat.
6. Use a little butter or cooking spray to grease the pan.
7. Pour about 1/4 cup of batter into the middle of the pan. Tilt and swirl the pan to spread the batter evenly into a thin circle.
8. Cook the crêpe for about one to two minutes, or until the sides start to lift and the bottom is golden brown.
9. Turn the crêpe over and cook for another 1–2 minutes.
10. Repeat with the rest of the dough, greasing the pan as necessary.
11. Sprinkle powdered sugar on the crêpes.
12. Serve the Orange and Grand Marnier Crêpes hot.

GAUFRES AU CITRON (LEMON WAFFLES):

INGREDIENTS:
- 2 cups all-purpose flour
- 1/4 cup granulated sugar
- 1 tablespoon baking powder
- 1/2 teaspoon salt
- 2 large eggs
- 1 3/4 cups milk
- 1/2 cup unsalted butter, melted
- Zest of 2 lemons
- Juice of 1 lemon
- Powdered sugar for dusting

INSTRUCTIONS:
1. Whisk the flour, sugar, baking powder, and salt together in a bowl.
2. Mix the eggs, milk, melted butter, lemon zest, and lemon juice together in a different bowl until everything is well mixed.
3. Pour the egg and milk mixture into the flour mixture slowly while whisking. Keep whisking until you have a smooth batter.
4. Follow the directions on the box to heat up a waffle iron.
5. Use a little butter or cooking spray to grease the waffle pan.
6. Spoon some of the batter into the center of the waffle iron, which has already been heated, and spread it out a bit to cover the area.
7. Close the waffle maker and let it cook until golden brown and crisp.
8. Repeat with the rest of the dough.
9. Powdered sugar goes on top of the waffles.
10. The Gaufres au Citron should be served warm.

CRÊPES WITH CARAMELIZED APPLES AND CINNAMON:

INGREDIENTS:

- 1 cup all-purpose flour
- 2 tablespoons granulated sugar
- 1/4 teaspoon salt
- 3 large eggs
- 1 cup milk
- 2 tablespoons unsalted butter, melted
- 4 medium apples, peeled, cored, and thinly sliced
- 2 tablespoons unsalted butter
- 2 tablespoons brown sugar
- 1/2 teaspoon ground cinnamon
- Whipped cream or vanilla ice cream for serving (optional)

INSTRUCTIONS:

1. Whisk the flour, sugar, and salt together in a bowl.
2. In a different bowl, beat the eggs and milk together until they are well mixed.
3. Pour the egg and milk mixture into the flour mixture slowly while whisking. Keep whisking until you have a smooth batter.
4. Mix in the butter that has melted.
5. In a large pan, melt the butter over medium heat.
6. Add the apple slices, brown sugar, and cinnamon powder to the pan.
7. Cook, stirring every so often, for about 5–7 minutes, until the apples are soft and browned.
8. Heat a skillet or crêpe pan that doesn't stick over medium heat.
9. Use a little butter or cooking spray to grease the pan.
10. Pour about 1/4 cup of batter into the middle of the pan. Tilt and swirl the pan to spread the batter evenly into a thin circle.
11. Cook the crêpe for about one to two minutes, or until the sides start to lift and the bottom is golden brown.

12. Turn the crêpe over and cook for another 1–2 minutes.
13. Repeat with the rest of the dough, greasing the pan as necessary.
14. Serve each crêpe with a spoonful of caramelized apples and a dab of whipped cream or a scoop of vanilla ice cream, if you like.

BUCKWHEAT PANCAKES WITH SMOKED SALMON:

INGREDIENTS:
- 1 cup buckwheat flour
- 1/2 cup all-purpose flour
- 1/2 teaspoon salt
- 2 large eggs
- 2 cups buttermilk
- 2 tablespoons unsalted butter, melted
- 4 ounces of smoked salmon
- Fresh dill for garnish
- Sour cream or crème fraîche for serving

INSTRUCTIONS:
1. Mix the buckwheat, all-purpose, and salt in a bowl with a whisk.
2. In a different bowl, beat the eggs and add the buttermilk slowly while whisking until everything is well mixed.
3. Pour the egg and buttermilk mixture into the flour mixture slowly while whisking. Keep whisking until you have a smooth batter.
4. Give the batter about 10 minutes to rest.
5. Heat a non-stick pan or griddle over medium heat.
6. Use a small amount of butter or cooking spray to grease the pan.
7. Pour about 1/4 cup of batter into the pan and slightly spread it out to make a pancake.

8. Cook the pancake for about two to three minutes or until the top starts to get bubbles.
9. Flip the pancake and cook it on the other side for another 1–2 minutes.
10. Repeat with the rest of the batter, greasing the pan when necessary.
11. Serve each buckwheat pancake with smoked salmon, a sprinkle of fresh dill, and a dollop of sour cream or crème fraiche.

WAFFLES WITH CHOCOLATE GANACHE AND RASPBERRIES:

INGREDIENTS:
- 2 cups all-purpose flour
- 1/4 cup granulated sugar
- 1 tablespoon baking powder
- 1/2 teaspoon salt
- 2 large eggs
- 1 3/4 cups milk
- 1/2 cup unsalted butter, melted
- 1 cup semisweet chocolate chips
- 1/2 cup heavy cream
- Fresh raspberries for topping

INSTRUCTIONS:
1. Whisk the flour, sugar, baking powder, and salt together in a bowl.
2. Whisk the eggs, milk, and melted butter together in a different bowl until they are well mixed.
3. Pour the egg and milk mixture into the flour mixture slowly while whisking. Keep whisking until you have a smooth batter.
4. Follow the directions on the box to heat up a waffle iron.
5. Use a little butter or cooking spray to grease the waffle pan.

6. Spoon some of the batter into the center of the waffle iron, which has already been heated, and spread it out a bit to cover the area.
7. Close the waffle maker and let it cook until golden brown and crisp.
8. Repeat with the rest of the dough.
9. Heat the heavy cream in a small pot until it starts to bubble.
10. Take the pan off the heat and put the chocolate chips in it.
11. Let the chocolate chips sit in the hot cream for a minute to make chocolate ganache, then mix until smooth and shiny.
12. Pour some chocolate ganache over the waffles and top them with fresh strawberries.

CRÊPES WITH NUTELLA AND BANANAS:

INGREDIENTS:
- 1 cup all-purpose flour
- 2 tablespoons granulated sugar
- 1/4 teaspoon salt
- 3 large eggs
- 1 cup milk
- 2 tablespoons unsalted butter, melted
- Nutella (chocolate hazelnut spread) for filling
- Sliced bananas for topping

INSTRUCTIONS:
1. Whisk the flour, sugar, and salt together in a bowl.
2. In a different bowl, beat the eggs and milk together until they are well mixed.
3. Pour the egg and milk mixture into the flour mixture slowly while whisking. Keep whisking until you have a smooth batter.
4. Mix in the butter that has melted.
5. Heat a skillet or crêpe pan that doesn't stick over medium heat.
6. Use a little butter or cooking spray to grease the pan.

7. Pour about 1/4 cup of batter into the middle of the pan. Tilt and swirl the pan to spread the batter evenly into a thin circle.
8. Cook the crêpe for about one to two minutes, or until the sides start to lift and the bottom is golden brown.
9. Turn the crêpe over and cook for another 1–2 minutes.
10. Repeat with the rest of the dough, greasing the pan as necessary.
11. On one half of each crêpe, spread a thin layer of Nutella.
12. On top of the Nutella, put slices of banana.
13. Fold the crêpe in half, then in half again to make a triangle.
14. Warm the crêpes and serve them with Nutella and bananas.

ALMOND FLOUR PANCAKES WITH BERRIES:

INGREDIENTS:
- 1 cup almond flour
- 1/4 cup all-purpose flour
- 1 tablespoon granulated sugar
- 1/2 teaspoon baking powder
- 1/4 teaspoon salt
- 2 large eggs
- 1/2 cup milk
- 1 teaspoon vanilla extract
- Fresh berries for topping

INSTRUCTIONS:
1. Mix the almond flour, all-purpose flour, sugar, baking powder, and salt in a bowl with a whisk.
2. Whisk the eggs, milk, and vanilla extract together in a different bowl until they are well mixed.
3. Pour the egg and milk mixture into the flour mixture slowly while whisking. Keep whisking until you have a smooth batter.
4. Heat a non-stick pan or griddle over medium heat.

5. Use a small amount of butter or cooking spray to grease the pan.
6. Pour about 1/4 cup of batter into the pan and slightly spread it out to make a pancake.
7. Cook the pancake for about two to three minutes or until the top starts to get bubbles.
8. Flip the pancake and cook it on the other side for another 1–2 minutes.
9. Repeat with the rest of the batter, greasing the pan when necessary.
10. Serve the pancakes on a plate with fresh berries on top.

WAFFLES WITH MAPLE SYRUP AND BACON:

INGREDIENTS:
- 2 cups all-purpose flour
- 1/4 cup granulated sugar
- 1 tablespoon baking powder
- 1/2 teaspoon salt
- 2 large eggs
- 1 3/4 cups milk
- 1/2 cup unsalted butter, melted
- Maple syrup for topping
- Cooked bacon for topping

INSTRUCTIONS:
1. Whisk the flour, sugar, baking powder, and salt together in a bowl.
2. Whisk the eggs, milk, and melted butter together in a different bowl until they are well mixed.
3. Pour the egg and milk mixture into the flour mixture slowly while whisking. Keep whisking until you have a smooth batter.
4. Follow the directions on the box to heat up a waffle iron.
5. Use a little butter or cooking spray to grease the waffle pan.

6. Spoon some of the batter into the center of the waffle iron, which has already been heated, and spread it out a bit to cover the area.
7. Close the waffle maker and let it cook until golden brown and crisp.
8. Repeat with the rest of the dough.
9. Serve the waffles with maple syrup drizzled on top and chopped cooked bacon.

CRÊPES WITH LEMON AND SUGAR:

INGREDIENTS:
- 1 cup all-purpose flour
- 2 tablespoons granulated sugar
- 1/4 teaspoon salt
- 3 large eggs
- 1 cup milk
- 2 tablespoons unsalted butter, melted
- Freshly squeezed lemon juice
- Granulated sugar for sprinkling

INSTRUCTIONS:
1. Whisk the flour, sugar, and salt together in a bowl.
2. In a different bowl, beat the eggs and milk until they are well mixed.
3. Pour the egg and milk mixture into the flour mixture slowly while whisking. Keep whisking until you have a smooth batter.
4. Mix in the butter that has melted.
5. Heat a skillet or crêpe pan that doesn't stick over medium heat.
6. Use a little butter or cooking spray to grease the pan.
7. Pour about 1/4 cup of batter into the middle of the pan. Tilt and swirl the pan to spread the batter evenly into a thin circle.
8. Cook the crêpe for about one to two minutes, or until the sides start to lift and the bottom is golden brown.

9. Turn the crêpe over and cook for another 1–2 minutes.
10. Repeat with the rest of the dough, greasing the pan as necessary.
11. Fresh lemon juice should be squeezed over each crêpe, and powdered sugar should be sprinkled on top.
12. Fold the crêpes in half, then in half again to make a triangle.
13. Serve the crêpes hot with sugar and lemon.

CHOCOLATE WAFFLES WITH WHIPPED CREAM:

INGREDIENTS:
- 2 cups all-purpose flour
- 1/4 cup cocoa powder
- 1/4 cup granulated sugar
- 1 tablespoon baking powder
- 1/2 teaspoon salt
- 2 large eggs
- 1 3/4 cups milk
- 1/2 cup unsalted butter, melted
- Whipped cream for topping
- Chocolate shavings for garnish

INSTRUCTIONS:
1. Mix the flour, cocoa powder, sugar, baking powder, and salt in a bowl with a whisk.
2. Whisk the eggs, milk, and melted butter together in a different bowl until they are well mixed.
3. Pour the egg and milk mixture into the flour mixture slowly while whisking. Keep whisking until you have a smooth batter.
4. Follow the directions on the box to heat up a waffle iron.
5. Use a little butter or cooking spray to grease the waffle pan.
6. Spoon some of the batter into the center of the waffle iron, which has already been heated, and spread it out a bit to cover the area.

7. Close the waffle maker and let it cook until golden brown and crisp.
8. Repeat with the rest of the dough.
9. Serve the chocolate waffles with whipped cream on top and chocolate shavings around the edge.

CHAPTER:10
PUFF PASTRY DESSERTS

MILLE-FEUILLE (NAPOLEON):

INGREDIENTS:
- 1 package (17.3 ounces) puff pastry sheets, thawed
- 2 cups heavy cream
- 1/4 cup powdered sugar
- 1 teaspoon vanilla extract
- Fresh berries for garnish
- Powdered sugar for dusting

INSTRUCTIONS:
1. Turn the oven on and set it to 400°F (200°C).
2. Unfold each sheet of puff pastry and cut it into three equal squares.
3. Put the squares of puff pastry on a baking sheet that has been covered with parchment paper.
4. Prick the squares of puff pastry all over with a fork to stop them from rising too much.
5. Bake the puff pastry in an oven that has been warm for about 15 to 20 minutes or until it is golden brown and puffy.
6. Take the puff pastry pieces out of the oven and let them cool all the way down.
7. Heavy cream, powdered sugar, and vanilla extract should be whipped together in a bowl until stiff peaks form.

8. Put one square of puff pastry on a plate and spread whipped cream.
9. Use more puff pastry and whipped cream to make another layer.
10. Put the last puff pastry square on top.
11. Sprinkle powdered sugar on top and decorate with fresh berries.
12. Before serving, put it in the fridge for at least an hour to set the layers.

TARTE AUX POMMES (APPLE TART):

INGREDIENTS:

- 1 sheet of puff pastry, thawed
- 3-4 apples, peeled, cored, and thinly sliced
- 2 tablespoons granulated sugar
- 1 teaspoon ground cinnamon
- 2 tablespoons unsalted butter, melted
- Apricot jam (optional)
- Powdered sugar for dusting

INSTRUCTIONS:

1. Turn the oven on and set it to 400°F (200°C).
2. On a lightly floured surface, roll out the puff pastry sheet into a rectangle.
3. Place the puff pastry on parchment paper on a baking sheet.
4. Set the apple slices on top of the puff pastry so that they meet and leave a border around the edges.
5. Mix the powdered sugar and ground cinnamon in a small bowl.
6. The cinnamon and sugar mixture should be sprinkled over the apple pieces.
7. Pour the butter that has been melted over the apples.
8. Bake for about 20 to 25 minutes in an oven that has already been warmed or until the puff pastry is golden brown and the apples are soft.

9. Take the tart out of the oven and let it cool down a bit.
10. If you want the apples to look shiny, you can heat a small amount of apricot jam and brush it over them.
11. Before you serve the tart, dust it with powdered sugar.

PITHIVIERS (ALMOND CREAM PUFF PASTRY):

INGREDIENTS:
- 1 sheet of puff pastry, thawed
- 1 cup almond flour
- 1/2 cup granulated sugar
- 1/4 cup unsalted butter, softened
- 2 large eggs
- 1/2 teaspoon almond extract
- Powdered sugar for dusting

INSTRUCTIONS:
1. Turn the oven on and set it to 400°F (200°C).
2. Roll out the puff pastry sheet into a circle on a surface with just a little bit of flour on it.
3. Place the puff pastry on parchment paper on a baking sheet.
4. Mix the almond flour, sugar, softened butter, eggs, and almond flavor in a bowl until everything is well blended.
5. Spread the almond mixture evenly in the middle of the puff pastry, leaving a line around the edges.
6. To cover the almond mixture, fold the puff pastry in half and press the sides together to seal.
7. Use a knife to make a design on top of the pastry to make it look nice.
8. Bake in a warm oven for 20 to 25 minutes or until the puff pastry is golden brown and the almond filling is set.
9. Take the Pithiviers out of the oven and let them cool down a bit.
10. Before you serve it, dust it with powdered sugar.

CHERRY AND CREAM CHEESE DANISH:

INGREDIENTS:

- 1 sheet of puff pastry, thawed
- 4 ounces cream cheese, softened
- 2 tablespoons granulated sugar
- 1/2 teaspoon vanilla extract
- Cherry pie filling or fresh cherries
- 1 egg, beaten (for egg wash)
- Powdered sugar for dusting

INSTRUCTIONS:

1. Turn the oven on and set it to 400°F (200°C).
2. Roll out the puff pastry sheet into a rectangle on a lightly floured surface.
3. Cut the sheet of puff pastry into smaller pieces or rectangles.
4. Mix the cream cheese, sugar, and vanilla extract in a bowl until they are smooth.
5. Each rectangle or square of puff pastry should have a spoonful of the cream cheese mixture spread on it.
6. On top of the cream cheese, put a spoonful of cherry pie filling or real cherries.
7. Fold the puff pastry's edges in toward the middle to make a ring around the filling.
8. For a golden finish, brush the sides of the pastry with beaten egg.
9. Bake the puff pastry in an oven that has been warm for about 15 to 20 minutes or until it is golden brown and puffy.
10. Take the danishes out of the oven and let them cool slightly.
11. Before you serve it, dust it with powdered sugar.

FRENCH PALMIERS:

INGREDIENTS:
- 1 sheet of puff pastry, thawed
- Granulated sugar

INSTRUCTIONS:
1. Turn the oven on and set it to 400°F (200°C).
2. Roll out the puff pastry sheet into a rectangle on a lightly floured surface.
3. Sprinkle a lot of white sugar over the puff pastry's whole surface.
4. Roll the puff pastry tightly from one side to the middle, stopping in the middle.
5. Repeat the rolling process on the other side until the two rolls meet in the middle.
6. Cut the rolled puff pastry into pieces that are 1/2 inch thick.
7. Place the palmier slices, cut side down, on a baking sheet covered with parchment paper.
8. Press down gently on each slice to make it a little flatter.
9. Bake the palmiers in an oven that has already been hot for 12 to 15 minutes or until they are golden brown and caramelized.
10. Take the palmiers out of the oven and let them cool all the way down.

PUFF PASTRY SWIRLS WITH CHOCOLATE AND HAZELNUTS:

INGREDIENTS:
- 1 sheet of puff pastry, thawed
- Nutella (chocolate hazelnut spread)
- Crushed hazelnuts
- Powdered sugar for dusting

INSTRUCTIONS:
1. Turn the oven on and set it to 400°F (200°C).
2. On a lightly floured surface, roll out the puff pastry sheet into a rectangle.
3. Spread a thin layer of Nutella evenly over the whole puff pastry.
4. On top of the Nutella, sprinkle some crushed hazelnuts.
5. Roll the puff pastry into a log by tightly rolling it up from one end.
6. Cut the log into spirals that are 1/2 inch thick.
7. Cut side down, put the swirls on a baking sheet lined with parchment paper.
8. Bake for about 15 to 20 minutes in an oven that has already been warm or until the swirls are golden brown and puffed.
9. Take the swirls out of the oven and let them cool down a bit.
10. Before you serve it, dust it with powdered sugar.

APPLE AND CINNAMON TURNOVERS:

INGREDIENTS:
- 1 sheet of puff pastry, thawed
- 2 cups apples, peeled, cored, and diced
- 2 tablespoons granulated sugar
- 1/2 teaspoon ground cinnamon
- 1 tablespoon unsalted butter
- 1 egg, beaten (for egg wash)
- Powdered sugar for dusting

INSTRUCTIONS:
1. Turn the oven on and set it to 400°F (200°C).
2. Roll out the puff pastry sheet into a rectangle on a lightly floured surface.
3. Cut the sheet of puff pastry into pieces.
4. Melt the butter in a pan over medium heat.
5. Put the chopped apples, sugar, and cinnamon powder in the pan.
6. Cook, stirring occasionally, for about 5–7 minutes, until the apples are soft and browned.
7. Put a spoonful of the apples caramelized on one-half of each square of puff pastry.
8. To make a triangle form, fold the puff pastry over the filling.
9. Use a fork to seal the turnovers by pressing the edges together.
10. For a golden finish, brush the turnovers with beaten egg.
11. Put the tarts on a parchment-lined baking sheet.
12. Bake the turnovers in an oven that has been warm for about 15 to 20 minutes or until golden brown and puffed.
13. Take the tarts out of the oven and let them cool down.
14. Before you serve it, dust it with powdered sugar.

CHOCOLATE AND ALMOND CROISSANTS:

INGREDIENTS:
- 1 sheet of puff pastry, thawed
- Nutella (chocolate hazelnut spread)
- Sliced almonds
- Powdered sugar for dusting

INSTRUCTIONS:
1. Turn the oven on and set it to 400°F (200°C).
2. Roll out the puff pastry sheet into a rectangle on a lightly floured surface.
3. Cut squares out of the puff pastry sheet.
4. On the wide end of each triangle, spread a layer of Nutella.
5. Sliced nuts should be put on top of the Nutella.
6. Roll each triangle from the wide end toward the pointy end to make a croissant shape.
7. Put the pointy side down of the croissants on a baking sheet lined with parchment paper.
8. Bake the croissants in an oven that has been warm for about 15 to 20 minutes or until they are golden brown and puffed.
9. Take the croissants out of the oven and let them cool down a bit.
10. Before you serve it, dust it with powdered sugar.

PUFF PASTRY TWISTS WITH ORANGE ZEST:

INGREDIENTS:
- 1 sheet of puff pastry, thawed
- 1/4 cup granulated sugar
- Zest of 1 orange

INSTRUCTIONS:
1. Turn the oven on and set it to 400°F (200°C).
2. Roll out the puff pastry sheet into a rectangle on a lightly floured surface.
3. Mix the granulated sugar and orange juice in a small bowl.
4. Spread the orange sugar mixture all over the puff pastry in an even layer.
5. Use a rolling pin to gently press the sugar mixture into the puff pastry.
6. Make thin strips out of the puff dough.
7. Twist each strip so that it forms a coil.
8. Put the twists on a baking sheet that has been covered in parchment paper.
9. Bake the twists in an oven that has been warm for 12 to 15 minutes or until they are golden brown and puffed.
10. Take the twists out of the oven and let them cool down a bit.

RASPBERRY AND CREAM CHEESE PUFF PASTRY BRAID:

INGREDIENTS:
- 1 sheet of puff pastry, thawed
- 4 ounces cream cheese, softened
- 2 tablespoons granulated sugar
- 1/2 teaspoon vanilla extract
- 1 cup fresh raspberries
- 1 egg, beaten (for egg wash)
- Powdered sugar for dusting

INSTRUCTIONS:
1. Turn the oven on and set it to 400°F (200°C).
2. Roll out the puff pastry sheet into a rectangle on a lightly floured surface.
3. Mix the cream cheese, sugar, and vanilla extract in a bowl until they are smooth.
4. The cream cheese mixture should be spread in a vertical line down the middle of the puff pastry.
5. Fresh cherries go on top of the cream cheese mix.
6. Cut slits at an angle about 1 inch apart on both sides of the puff pastry.
7. Fold the dough strips over the filling to make a braided look, switching sides each time.
8. For a golden finish, brush the dough with beaten egg.
9. Place the braid on parchment paper on a baking sheet.
10. Bake the puff pastry in an oven that has already been warm for about 20 to 25 minutes or until golden brown and puffy.
11. Take the braid out of the oven and let it cool down a bit.
12. Before you serve it, dust it with powdered sugar.

PUFF PASTRY TART WITH CARAMELIZED ONIONS AND GOAT CHEESE:

INGREDIENTS:
- 1 sheet of puff pastry, thawed
- 2 large onions, thinly sliced
- 2 tablespoons unsalted butter
- 1 tablespoon balsamic vinegar
- 4 ounces goat cheese, crumbled
- Fresh thyme leaves
- Salt and pepper to taste

INSTRUCTIONS:
1. Turn the oven on and set it to 400°F (200°C).
2. Roll out the puff pastry sheet into a rectangle on a lightly floured surface.
3. Melt the butter in a pan over medium heat.
4. Add the sliced onions to the pan and cook, stirring every so often, for about 20 to 25 minutes, until the onions are cooked and golden brown.
5. Add the balsamic vinegar, stir, and cook for another 1–2 minutes.
6. Put the caramelized onions on the puff pastry, leaving a line around the edges.
7. Crumble the goat cheese on top of the onions.
8. Use salt, pepper, and fresh thyme leaves to season the food.
9. Fold the puff pastry's edges in toward the middle to make a ring around the filling.
10. Put the tart on parchment paper on a baking sheet.
11. Bake the puff pastry in an oven that has already been warm for about 20 to 25 minutes or until it is golden brown and puffy.
12. Take the tart out of the oven and let it cool a little bit before you serve it.

ALMOND AND PEAR TART IN PUFF PASTRY:

INGREDIENTS:
- 1 sheet of puff pastry, thawed
- 2 ripe pears, peeled, cored, and thinly sliced
- 1/4 cup granulated sugar
- 1/2 teaspoon almond extract
- 1/2 cup almond flour
- 2 tablespoons unsalted butter, melted
- Sliced almonds for topping
- Powdered sugar for dusting

INSTRUCTIONS:
1. Turn the oven on and set it to 400°F (200°C).
2. Roll out the puff pastry sheet into a rectangle on a lightly floured surface.
3. Mix the sliced pears, granulated sugar, and almond flavor together in a bowl.
4. Mix the almond flour and melted butter in a different bowl until they are well mixed.
5. Spread the almond flour mixture evenly on the puff pastry, leaving a line around the edges.
6. Place the sliced pears on top of the almond flour mixture.
7. Sliced nuts should be put on top of the pears.
8. Fold the puff pastry's edges in toward the middle to make a ring around the filling.
9. Put the tart on parchment paper on a baking sheet.
10. Bake the puff pastry in an oven that has already been warm for about 20 to 25 minutes or until it is golden brown and puffy.
11. Take the tart out of the oven and let it cool down a bit.
12. Before you serve it, dust it with powdered sugar.

PUFF PASTRY PINWHEELS WITH SPINACH AND RICOTTA:

INGREDIENTS:

- 1 sheet of puff pastry, thawed
- 1 cup fresh spinach leaves, chopped
- 1/2 cup ricotta cheese
- 1/4 cup grated Parmesan cheese
- 1 egg, beaten
- Salt and pepper to taste

INSTRUCTIONS:

1. Turn the oven on and set it to 400°F (200°C).
2. Roll out the puff pastry sheet into a rectangle on a lightly floured surface.
3. Mix chopped spinach, ricotta cheese, grated Parmesan cheese, an egg that has been whipped, salt, and pepper in a bowl.
4. Spread the spinach and ricotta mixture on the puff pastry evenly, leaving a line around the edges.
5. Roll the puff pastry into a log by tightly rolling it up from one end.
6. Cut the log into pieces about 1/2 inch thick.
7. Put the cut sides of the pinwheels down on a baking sheet lined with parchment paper.
8. Bake the pinwheels in an oven that has been warm for about 15 to 20 minutes or until they are golden brown and puffed.
9. Take the pinwheels out of the oven and let them cool a little bit before you serve them.

PLUM AND ALMOND PUFF PASTRY TART:

INGREDIENTS:
- 1 sheet of puff pastry, thawed
- 4-5 plums, pitted and sliced
- 2 tablespoons granulated sugar
- 1/2 teaspoon almond extract
- 1/4 cup almond flour
- Sliced almonds for topping
- Powdered sugar for dusting

INSTRUCTIONS:
1. Turn the oven on and set it to 400°F (200°C).
2. Roll out the puff pastry sheet into a rectangle on a lightly floured surface.
3. Mix the sliced plums with the granulated sugar and almond flavor in a bowl.
4. Spread the almond flour on the puff pastry in an even layer, leaving a line around the edges.
5. Place the plum slices on the almond flour.
6. Sliced almonds go on top of the plums.
7. Fold the puff pastry's edges in toward the middle to make a ring around the filling.
8. Put the tart on parchment paper on a baking sheet.
9. Bake the puff pastry in an oven that has already been warm for about 20 to 25 minutes or until it is golden brown and puffy.
10. Take the tart out of the oven and let it cool down a bit.
11. Before you serve it, dust it with powdered sugar.

CHOCOLATE AND RASPBERRY PUFF PASTRY TARTS:

INGREDIENTS:
- 1 sheet of puff pastry, thawed
- 1/2 cup semisweet chocolate chips
- 1/2 cup fresh raspberries
- 1 egg, beaten (for egg wash)
- Powdered sugar for dusting

INSTRUCTIONS:
1. Turn the oven on and set it to 400°F (200°C).
2. Roll out the puff pastry sheet into a rectangle on a lightly floured surface.
3. Cube or circle the puff dough into smaller pieces.
4. Put a spoonful of chocolate chips in the middle of each square or circle of puff pastry.
5. Fresh raspberries go on top of the chocolate chips.
6. Fold the puff pastry's edges in toward the middle to make a ring around the filling.
7. For a golden finish, brush the dough with beaten egg.
8. Put the tarts on a baking sheet that has been covered in parchment paper.
9. Bake the puff pastry in an oven that has been warm for about 15 to 20 minutes or until it is golden brown and puffy.
10. Take the tarts out of the oven and let them cool down a bit.
11. Before you serve it, dust it with powdered sugar.

CHAPTER:11
TARTS

TARTE AU CITRON (LEMON TART):

INGREDIENTS:
- 1 pre-baked tart shell (made with sweet shortcrust pastry)
- 3-4 large lemons, zest and juice
- 4 large eggs
- 1 cup granulated sugar
- 1/2 cup unsalted butter, melted

INSTRUCTIONS:
1. Preheat the oven to 350°F (175°C).
2. In a bowl, whisk together the eggs and sugar until well combined.
3. Add the lemon zest and juice to the egg mixture and whisk until smooth.
4. Slowly pour in the melted butter while whisking continuously.
5. Pour the lemon filling into the pre-baked tart shell.
6. Bake in the preheated oven for about 20-25 minutes or until the filling is set and slightly golden.
7. Remove from the oven and let the tart cool completely before serving.
8. Optional: Dust with powdered sugar or top with whipped cream before serving.

TARTE AUX FRAISES (STRAWBERRY TART):

INGREDIENTS:
- 1 pre-baked tart shell (made with sweet shortcrust pastry)
- Fresh strawberries, hulled and sliced
- 1/2 cup strawberry jam or glaze
- Whipped cream or vanilla ice cream (for serving)

INSTRUCTIONS:
1. Put the sliced strawberries in the tart shell that has already been baked.
2. Heat the strawberry jam or glaze over low heat in a small pot until it becomes liquid.
3. Brush the liquid jam or glaze over the strawberries to make a shiny glaze.
4. Put the tart in the fridge for at least an hour so the flavors blend and the glaze harden.
5. Serve cold with a dab of whipped cream or a scoop of vanilla ice cream.

FRENCH CHOCOLATE TART:

INGREDIENTS:
- 1 pre-baked tart shell (made with chocolate shortcrust pastry)
- 8 ounces dark chocolate, chopped
- 1 cup heavy cream
- 2 tablespoons unsalted butter
- Pinch of salt

INSTRUCTIONS:
1. Put the chopped dark chocolate in a bowl that can take the heat.

2. Heavy cream and butter should be heated over medium heat in a pot until it starts to simmer.
3. Pour the hot cream mixture over the chopped chocolate and let it sit for a minute to let the chocolate melt.
4. Add a pinch of salt and mix the ingredients until they are smooth and shiny.
5. Pour the chocolate filling into the tart shell that has already been baked.
6. Put the tart in the fridge for at least two hours or until the filling is firm.
7. Serve cold, and you can add cocoa powder or whipped cream if you want.

TARTE NORMANDE (NORMANDY APPLE TART):

INGREDIENTS:
- 1 pre-baked tart shell (made with sweet shortcrust pastry)
- 4-5 medium apples, peeled, cored, and thinly sliced
- 1/2 cup granulated sugar
- 2 tablespoons all-purpose flour
- 1/2 teaspoon ground cinnamon
- 1/4 teaspoon ground nutmeg
- 2 large eggs
- 1/2 cup heavy cream
- 1/2 teaspoon vanilla extract

INSTRUCTIONS:
1. Turn the oven on and set it to 375°F (190°C).
2. Mix the sliced apples, sugar, flour, cinnamon, and nutmeg in a bowl.
3. Place the apple mixture in the tart shell that has already been baked.
4. Whisk the eggs, heavy cream, and vanilla extract together in a separate bowl.
5. Pour the egg mixture on top of the apples in the tart shell.

6. Bake in an oven that has already been warm for 30 to 35 minutes, or until the apples are soft and the custard has set.
7. Take the tart out of the oven and let it cool a little bit before you serve it.
8. Optional: You can sprinkle powdered sugar on top or serve with vanilla ice cream.

TARTE AUX MYRTILLES (BLUEBERRY TART):

INGREDIENTS:

- 1 pre-baked tart shell (made with sweet shortcrust pastry)
- 2 cups fresh blueberries
- 1/2 cup granulated sugar
- 2 tablespoons cornstarch
- 1 tablespoon lemon juice
- Zest of 1 lemon

INSTRUCTIONS:

1. Put 1 cup of blueberries, sugar, cornstarch, lemon juice, and lemon zest into a pot.
2. Stir the blueberry mixture often while cooking it over medium heat until it thickens and the berries start to burst.
3. Take the blueberry blend off the stove and let it cool down a bit.
4. Spread the last cup of fresh blueberries evenly in the tart shell that has already been baked.
5. Pour the blueberry sauce cooked over the fresh blueberries, making sure to spread it out evenly.
6. Put the tart in the fridge for at least two hours or until the filling is firm.
7. Serve cold, with a sprinkle of powdered sugar or a dollop of whipped cream, if you like.

TARTE AU FROMAGE BLANC (WHITE CHEESE TART):

INGREDIENTS:

- 1 pre-baked tart shell (made with sweet shortcrust pastry)
- 2 cups fromage blanc or ricotta cheese
- 1/2 cup granulated sugar
- 2 large eggs
- 1 tablespoon all-purpose flour
- 1 teaspoon vanilla extract
- Zest of 1 lemon

INSTRUCTIONS:

1. Turn the oven on and set it to 350°F (175°C).
2. Put the fromage blanc or ricotta cheese, sugar, eggs, flour, vanilla extract, and lemon zest in a bowl and mix them.
3. Pour the cheese mix into the tart shell that has already been baked.
4. Bake for about 25 to 30 minutes in an oven that has already been warmed or until the filling is set and a little bit golden.
5. Take the tart out of the oven and let it cool down before serving it.
6. Optional: Before serving, sprinkle with powdered sugar or put fresh berries on top.

TARTE FLAMBÉE (ALSATIAN FLATBREAD TART):

INGREDIENTS:
- 1 pre-baked tart shell (made with thin pizza dough or bread dough)
- 1/2 cup crème fraîche or sour cream
- 1 large onion, thinly sliced
- 4-6 slices of bacon, cooked and crumbled
- Salt and pepper to taste

INSTRUCTIONS:
1. Set the oven temperature to 450°F (230°C).
2. Make a thin round form with the pizza dough or bread dough.
3. Spread a thin layer of crème fraiche or sour cream over the tart shell in an even layer.
4. On top of the crème fraiche, put the thinly sliced onions and chopped bacon.
5. Add salt and pepper to taste.
6. Bake for 10 to 15 minutes in an oven that has already been heated or until the base is crisp and the toppings are done.
7. Take the tart out of the oven and let it cool a little bit before you serve it.
8. Slice into thin pieces and serve hot.

PEAR AND FRANGIPANE TART:

INGREDIENTS:
- 1 pre-baked tart shell (made with sweet shortcrust pastry)
- 2-3 ripe pears, peeled, cored, and thinly sliced
- 1/2 cup almond flour
- 1/4 cup granulated sugar
- 4 tablespoons unsalted butter, softened
- 1 large egg
- 1 teaspoon vanilla extract

- Powdered sugar for dusting

INSTRUCTIONS:

1. Turn the oven on and set it to 375°F (190°C).
2. Mix the almond flour, sugar, melted butter, egg, and vanilla extract in a bowl until they are well mixed.
3. Spread the almond frangipane mixture evenly on the tart shell that has already been baked.
4. Place the pear slices on the frangipane and lightly press them into the filling.
5. Bake in an oven that has already been warm for about 30–35 minutes, or until the pears are soft and the filling is golden brown.
6. Take the tart out of the oven and let it cool a little bit before you serve it.
7. Before you serve it, dust it with powdered sugar.

CHOCOLATE AND SALTED CARAMEL TART:

INGREDIENTS:

- 1 pre-baked tart shell (made with chocolate shortcrust pastry)
- 8 ounces dark chocolate, chopped
- 1/2 cup heavy cream
- 2 tablespoons unsalted butter
- 1/2 cup granulated sugar
- 1/4 cup water
- Sea salt or fleur de sel for sprinkling

INSTRUCTIONS:

1. Put the chopped dark chocolate in a bowl that can take the heat.
2. Heavy cream and butter should be heated over medium heat in a pot until it simmer.

3. Pour the hot cream mixture over the chopped chocolate and let it sit for a minute to let the chocolate melt.
4. Mix it until it is smooth and shiny.
5. Pour the chocolate filling into the tart shell that has already been baked, and then smooth the top.
6. In a different pot, mix the granulated sugar and water.
7. Stir the sugar mixture occasionally as you cook it over medium heat until it turns amber and makes a caramel.
8. Pour the salted caramel over the chocolate filling and swirl it around with a spoon or stick to make it look like it's marbled.
9. Salt the top of the tart with sea salt or fleur de sel.
10. Put the tart in the fridge for at least two hours or until the filling is firm.
11. Serve cold, and add whipped cream or cocoa powder if you want.

FRESH FIG AND ALMOND TART:

INGREDIENTS:
- 1 pre-baked tart shell (made with sweet shortcrust pastry)
- 10-12 fresh figs, stemmed and halved
- 1/2 cup almond flour
- 1/4 cup granulated sugar
- 4 tablespoons unsalted butter, softened
- 1 large egg
- 1 teaspoon almond extract
- Sliced almonds for topping
- Honey for drizzling

INSTRUCTIONS:
1. Turn the oven on and set it to 375°F (190°C).
2. Cream the almond flour, sugar, softened butter, egg, and almond flavor together until everything is well mixed.
3. Spread the nut mixture evenly on the tart shell that has already been baked.

4. Place the figs halves on top of the nut mixture and lightly press them into the filling.
5. Sliced nuts go on top of the figs.
6. Bake in an oven that has already been warm for about 30–35 minutes, or until the figs are soft and the filling is golden brown.
7. Take the tart out of the oven and let it cool a little bit before you serve it.
8. Add honey right before serving.

TARTE À LA RHUBARBE (RHUBARB TART):

INGREDIENTS:
- 1 pre-baked tart shell (made with sweet shortcrust pastry)
- 2 cups rhubarb, cut into 1/2-inch pieces
- 1/2 cup granulated sugar
- 1/4 cup all-purpose flour
- 1/2 teaspoon ground cinnamon
- 1/4 teaspoon ground ginger
- 1/4 teaspoon ground nutmeg
- 1/4 teaspoon vanilla extract

INSTRUCTIONS:
1. Turn the oven on and set it to 375°F (190°C).
2. Mix the rhubarb, sugar, flour, cinnamon, ginger, nutmeg, and vanilla extract together in a bowl.
3. Spread the rhubarb mixture out evenly in the tart shell that has already been baked.
4. Bake for about 30–35 minutes in an oven that has already been heated or until the rhubarb is soft and the sauce is bubbling.
5. Take the tart out of the oven and let it cool a little bit before you serve it.
6. You can sprinkle powdered sugar on top or serve with vanilla ice cream.

TARTE AU CHOCOLAT BLANC (WHITE CHOCOLATE TART):

INGREDIENTS:

- 1 pre-baked tart shell (made with sweet shortcrust pastry)
- 8 ounces white chocolate, chopped
- 1 cup heavy cream
- 2 tablespoons unsalted butter
- 1 teaspoon vanilla extract
- Fresh berries for garnish

INSTRUCTIONS:

1. Put the chopped white chocolate in a bowl that can handle the heat.
2. Heavy cream and butter should be heated over medium heat in a pot until it starts to simmer.
3. Pour the hot cream mixture over the chopped white chocolate and let it sit for a minute to let the chocolate melt.
4. Stir the liquid until it is smooth and creamy, then add the vanilla extract.
5. Put the white chocolate filling into the tart shell that has already been baked.
6. Put the tart in the fridge for at least two hours or until the filling is firm.
7. Put fresh berries on top of the tart before you serve it.
8. Cool and serve.

RASPBERRY AND PISTACHIO TART:

INGREDIENTS:

- 1 pre-baked tart shell (made with sweet shortcrust pastry)
- 1 cup fresh raspberries
- 1/4 cup shelled pistachios, chopped
- 1/4 cup raspberry jam or glaze

INSTRUCTIONS:

1. Spread out the fresh strawberries on the tart shell that has already been baked.
2. Spritz the strawberries with the chopped pistachios.
3. Warm the raspberry jam or glaze over low heat in a small pot until it becomes liquid.
4. Brush the liquid jam or glaze over the raspberries to make a shiny glaze.
5. Put the tart in the fridge for at least an hour so the flavors blend and the glaze harden.
6. Cool and serve.

TARTE AU CHÈVRE ET MIEL (GOAT CHEESE AND HONEY TART):

INGREDIENTS:

- 1 pre-baked tart shell (made with savory shortcrust pastry)
- 6 ounces goat cheese, crumbled
- 2 tablespoons honey
- Fresh thyme leaves
- Salt and pepper to taste

INSTRUCTIONS:

1. Turn the oven on and set it to 375°F (190°C).
2. Spread the crumbled goat cheese out evenly in the tart shell that has already been baked.
3. Pour the honey over the goat cheese, spread it out evenly.
4. Sprinkle the tart with fresh thyme leaves, salt, and pepper.
5. Bake for 15 to 20 minutes in an oven that has already been warm or until the cheese has softened and turned a light golden color.
6. Take the tart out of the oven and let it cool a little bit before you serve it.
7. Serve at room temperature or warm.

TARTE AUX PRUNES (PLUM TART):

INGREDIENTS:
- 1 pre-baked tart shell (made with sweet shortcrust pastry)
- 4-5 plums, pitted and thinly sliced
- 1/4 cup granulated sugar
- 1 tablespoon all-purpose flour
- 1/2 teaspoon ground cinnamon
- 1/4 teaspoon almond extract
- Sliced almonds for topping

INSTRUCTIONS:
1. Turn the oven on and set it to 375°F (190°C).
2. Mix the sliced plums, sugar, flour, cinnamon, and almond flavor in a bowl.
3. Spread the plum mixture out evenly in the tart shell that has already been baked.
4. Sliced almonds go on top of the plums.
5. Bake for about 25 to 30 minutes in an oven that has already been warmed or until the plums are soft and the filling is golden.
6. Take the tart out of the oven and let it cool a little bit before you serve it.
7. Dust with powdered sugar before serving if you want.

CHAPTER:12
CANDIES AND MIGNARDISES

CHOCOLATE TRUFFLES WITH ORANGE LIQUEUR:

INGREDIENTS:
- 8 ounces dark chocolate, chopped
- 1/2 cup heavy cream
- 2 tablespoons unsalted butter
- 2 tablespoons orange liqueur (such as Grand Marnier or Cointreau)
- Cocoa powder or powdered sugar (for rolling)

INSTRUCTIONS:
1. Put the chopped dark chocolate in a bowl that can take the heat.
2. Heavy cream and butter should be heated over medium heat in a pot until it simmer.
3. Pour the hot cream mixture over the chopped chocolate and let it sit for a minute to let the chocolate melt.
4. Add the orange liquor and stir until everything is smooth and mixed well.
5. Cover the bowl with plastic wrap and put it in the fridge for about 2 hours or until the mixture is hard to handle.
6. Using a small spoon or a melon baller, scoop out small amounts of the chocolate mixture and roll them into small balls.
7. Roll them in cocoa powder or powdered sugar to coat the truffles equally.
8. Put the truffles with the coating on a baking sheet covered with parchment paper.
9. Set the truffles in the fridge for another 1–2 hours.
10. Serve at room temperature or cold.

CALISSONS D'AIX (ALMOND AND CANDIED FRUIT PASTE):

INGREDIENTS:

- 1 1/2 cups blanched almonds
- 1/2 cup powdered sugar
- 1/4 cup candied orange peel
- 1/4 cup candied melon peel
- 1/4 teaspoon almond extract
- 1/4 teaspoon orange blossom water
- 1 egg white
- Edible wafer paper (optional)
- Powdered sugar (for dusting)

INSTRUCTIONS:

1. Blend the blanched almonds and powdered sugar in a food processor until they are finely ground.
2. Add the candied orange peel, candied melon peel, almond flavor, and orange blossom water to the almond mixture. Process until the ingredients are well mixed and the mixture sticks together.
3. Add the egg white to the almond paste in a bowl. Stir the mixture until it becomes a smooth paste.
4. Sprinkle powdered sugar on a clean surface and roll out the .almond paste until it is about 1/4 inch thick.
5. Cut the almond paste that has been rolled out into diamond-shaped pieces.
6. Optional: On the bottom of each lesson, put a small piece of wafer paper that can be eaten.
7. Let the calissons dry for about 1 to 2 hours at room temperature.
8. Store in a cool, dry place in a container that keeps out air.

NOUGAT DE MONTÉLIMAR:

INGREDIENTS:

- 2 cups whole almonds
- 2 cups pistachios
- 1 cup honey
- 1 1/2 cups granulated sugar
- 3 large egg whites
- 1 teaspoon vanilla extract
- Edible rice paper (optional)

INSTRUCTIONS:

1. Turn the oven on and set it to 350°F (175°C). Almonds and walnuts should be spread out on a baking sheet and toasted in the oven for about 8 to 10 minutes or until they are lightly golden. Let them get cold.
2. Mix the honey and sugar together in a big pot. Stir while heating over medium heat until the sugar is dissolved. Bring the mixture to a boil and cook it until a candy thermometer reads soft-ball stage, which is about 250°F or 120°C.
3. Whisk the egg whites in a separate bowl until stiff peaks form.
4. Slowly pour the hot honey mixture into the egg whites that have been whisked. Keep mixing the whole time.
5. Keep mixing the mixture until it gets thick and shiny.
6. Add the toasted almonds, pistachios, and vanilla extract and stir until everything is well-mixed.
7. Using edible rice paper, line a rectangular baking dish, and pour the nougat mixture into the dish. Use a spoon to smooth the top.
8. Let the nougat cool at room temperature for several hours or overnight to make sure it is completely cool.
9. Cut the nougat into small pieces or rectangles after the nougat has cooled and hardened.
10. Store at room temperature in a jar that won't let air in.

FRENCH SALTED BUTTER CARAMELS:

INGREDIENTS:

- 1 cup heavy cream
- 1/2 cup unsalted butter
- 1 cup granulated sugar
- 1/2 cup light corn syrup
- 1/2 teaspoon sea salt
- Flaky sea salt (for topping)

INSTRUCTIONS:

1. Line a square 8-inch baking pan with parchment paper, leaving a little extra so it's easy to take out.
2. Heavy cream and butter should be mixed together in a pot. Melt the butter and heat the mixture over medium-low heat until it is hot. Take it off the heat and set it aside.
3. Mix the granulated sugar, corn syrup, and sea salt in a separate big saucepan. Cook the mixture over medium heat, turning it all the time, until a candy thermometer reads 250°F (120°C) (the "firm-ball stage").
4. Take the sugar mixture off the heat and, while stirring, slowly pour in the hot cream and butter mixture.
5. Return the pot to medium heat and stir the caramel constantly until a candy thermometer reads 245°F (118°C) (the "soft-ball stage").
6. Pour the caramel into the baking dish that has been set up. After a few minutes, sprinkle the top with flakes of sea salt.
7. Let the caramel cool completely at room temperature for a few hours or overnight.
8. Cut the caramel into small squares or shapes once the caramel has cooled and hardened.
9. Put wax paper or parchment paper around each caramel.
10. Store at room temperature in a jar that won't let air in.

PÂTE DE FRUITS (FRUIT JELLIES):

INGREDIENTS:
- 2 cups fruit puree (such as raspberry, strawberry, or apricot)
- 1/4 cup lemon juice
- 3 cups granulated sugar
- 1/2 cup liquid pectin
- Granulated sugar (for coating)

INSTRUCTIONS:
1. Mix the fruit puree, lemon juice, and sugar together in a pot. Stir constantly over medium heat until the sugar has dissolved.
2. Bring the mixture to a boil by turning up the heat to medium-high. Keep boiling and shaking the mixture every so often until a candy thermometer reads 223°F (106°C) (the gel stage).
3. Take the pan off the heat and stir the liquid pectin in quickly.
4. Pour the fruit mixture into a square 8-inch baking dish that has been oiled.
5. Let the mixture cool and set at room temperature for a few hours or overnight.
6. When the fruit jellies have set, cut them into small squares or circles.
7. Each fruit jelly should be rolled in fine sugar to cover all sides.
8. Store at room temperature in a jar that won't let air in.

DARK CHOCOLATE MENDIANTS:

INGREDIENTS:
- 8 ounces dark chocolate, chopped
- Assorted toppings (such as dried fruits, nuts, and seeds)

INSTRUCTIONS:
1. Put parchment paper on a baking sheet.

2. Melt the chopped dark chocolate in a bowl that can handle heat over a double boiler or in the microwave, stirring until it is smooth.
3. Drop spoonfuls of the melted chocolate onto the prepared baking sheet and spread them out into small circles or ovals.
4. Put different toppings on the chocolate rounds and gently press them into the chocolate to decorate them.
5. Let the chocolate mendiants cool down and set at room temperature for about an hour, or put them in the fridge if you want them to set faster.
6. Once the mendicants are set, take them off the parchment paper and keep them at room temperature in a container with a lid.

RASPBERRY MACARONS:

INGREDIENTS:
- 1 cup almond flour
- 1 3/4 cups powdered sugar
- 3 large egg whites
- 1/4 cup granulated sugar
- Red food coloring (optional)
- Raspberry jam or raspberry buttercream (for filling)

INSTRUCTIONS:
1. Mix the almond flour and powdered sugar together in a food processor. Mix and grind until everything is well mixed and fine.
2. Beat the egg whites in a bowl until they get foamy. Slowly add the granulated sugar until stiff peaks form as you continue to beat.
3. With a spoon, fold the almond flour mixture into the beaten egg whites until everything is mixed well. Add a few drops of red food coloring if you want it to be pink.
4. Put the dough into a piping bag with a round tip.

5. Pipe small rings of batter on a baking sheet covered with parchment paper. Give each macaron some space between them.
6. Tap the baking sheet a few times on the counter to eliminate any air bubbles and help the macarons spread out a bit.
7. Let the macarons sit at room temperature for about 30 minutes or until a skin forms on the top. This will help them get their distinctive "feet" as they bake.
8. Turn the oven on and set it to 300°F (150°C).
9. Bake the macarons in an oven that has been heated for about 15 to 18 minutes or until they are hard and set. Let them cool down completely on the baking sheet.
10. Once the shells have cooled, put the ones that are the same size together. Spoon a small amount of raspberry jam or raspberry frosting onto the flat side of one shell and place another shell on top.
11. Before serving, put the filled macarons in a container with a lid and put it in the fridge for at least 24 hours. This helps their taste and texture develop.

CHOCOLATE COVERED ORANGE PEELS:

INGREDIENTS:
- 2 oranges
- Water
- 1 cup granulated sugar
- 8 ounces dark chocolate, chopped

INSTRUCTIONS:
1. Peel the oranges and cut them into pieces.
2. Cut thin pieces from the orange peel.
3. Put the strips of orange peel in a pot and cover them with cold water. Bring to a boil and cook for about 5 minutes on low heat. Pour out the water and do this process twice more. This helps get rid of the bitter taste of the peel.

4. Mix the powdered sugar and 1 cup of water in the same pot. Bring to a boil and stir until the sugar is completely melted.
5. Add the strips of orange peel that have been washed and dried to the sugar syrup and let it cook for about 30 minutes or until the peel turns clear and soft.
6. Take the strips of orange peel out of the syrup and set them on a wire rack to cool.
7. Melt the chopped dark chocolate in a bowl that can handle heat over a double boiler or in the microwave, stirring until it is smooth.
8. Dip each orange peel strip partly or all the way through the melted chocolate. Put the chocolate-covered peel strips on a parchment paper-lined baking sheet.
9. Let the orange peels wrapped in chocolate cool and set at room temperature for about an hour, or put them in the fridge if you want them to set faster.
10. Once the chocolate is set, take the orange peels off the parchment paper and put them in a jar with a lid. Store them at room temperature.

LAVENDER HONEY FUDGE:

INGREDIENTS:
- 1 1/2 cups granulated sugar
- 1/2 cup unsalted butter
- 1/4 cup honey
- 2/3 cup heavy cream
- 1 tablespoon dried lavender buds (culinary grade)
- 1 teaspoon vanilla extract

INSTRUCTIONS:
1. Line a square baking dish that is 8 inches square with parchment paper.
2. Put the sugar, butter, honey, heavy cream, and dried lavender buds into a pot.

3. Stir the liquid constantly while heating it over medium heat until the sugar is dissolved and it comes to a gentle boil.
4. Keep boiling the mixture and stirring it often until it hits the soft-ball stage, which on a candy thermometer is about 240°F or 115°C.
5. Take the pan off the stove and let it cool down for a few minutes.
6. Add the vanilla extract and mix well.
7. Mix the ingredients with a wooden spoon or a hand mixer until they start to thicken and lose their shine.
8. Pour the fudge mixture into the pan that has been greased and use a spoon to smooth the top.
9. Let the fudge sit out at room temperature for a few hours or overnight to cool completely.
10. Once the lavender honey fudge has cooled and set, cut it into small pieces.
11. Store at room temperature in a jar that won't let air in.

PISTACHIO MARZIPAN:

INGREDIENTS:
- 1 1/2 cups blanched almonds
- 1 cup powdered sugar
- 1/4 cup granulated sugar
- 1/2 teaspoon almond extract
- Green food coloring (optional)
- 1/4 cup pistachios, finely chopped (for coating)

INSTRUCTIONS:
1. Blend the blanched almonds and powdered sugar in a food processor until they are finely ground.
2. Add the sugar and almond flavor to the mixture of almonds. Process until the ingredients are well mixed and the mixture sticks together.
3. You can add a few drops of green food coloring if you want a pistachio color.

4. Put the marzipan mixture on a clean surface and knead it until it is smooth and easy to shape.
5. The marzipan can be rolled into small balls or shaped into other shapes.
6. Finely chopped pistachios are used to cover the marzipan forms.
7. Let the pistachio marzipan dry at room temperature for about 1 to 2 hours.
8. Store at room temperature in a jar that won't let air in.

FRENCH ALMOND DRAGEES:

INGREDIENTS:
- 1 cup whole almonds
- 1 cup granulated sugar
- 1/4 cup water
- 1/4 teaspoon almond extract
- Food coloring (optional)

INSTRUCTIONS:
1. Mix the sugar and water together in a pot. Stir constantly over medium heat until the sugar has dissolved.
2. Bring the sugar syrup to a boil and cook it until a candy thermometer reads soft-ball stage, which is about 240°F or 115°C.
3. Take the pot off the heat, stir in the almond extract, and, if you want, a few drops of food coloring.
4. Pour the sugar syrup into a bowl and stir in the whole almonds to coat them evenly.
5. Place the covered almonds in a single layer on a baking sheet lined with parchment paper. Leave some space between them.
6. Let the almond dragees dry for a few hours or overnight at room temperature.
7. Once the almond dragees are dry, keep them at room temperature in a container that won't let air in.

LEMON MADELEINES:

INGREDIENTS:
- 2/3 cup all-purpose flour
- 1/2 teaspoon baking powder
- Pinch of salt
- 1/2 cup unsalted butter, melted and cooled
- 1/2 cup granulated sugar
- 2 large eggs
- 1 teaspoon vanilla extract
- Zest of 1 lemon

INSTRUCTIONS:
1. Turn the oven on and set it to 375°F (190°C). Use butter or food spray to grease a madeleine pan.
2. Mix the flour, baking powder, and salt in a small bowl with a whisk. Set aside.
3. Beat the melted butter and powdered sugar together in a bowl until they are well mixed.
4. Add the eggs one by one, mixing well after each one. Add the vanilla extract and lemon zest and stir again.
5. Gradually add the flour mixture to the wet ingredients and stir until just mixed.
6. Spoon the batter into the madeleine pan that has been prepared. Fill each shape about 3/4 of the way with batter.
7. Bake the madeleines in an oven that has already been warm for about 10 to 12 minutes, or until the edges are golden and they bounce back when lightly pressed.
8. Take the madeleines out of the pan and put them on a wire rack so they can cool.
9. When the madeleines have cooled, dust them with powdered sugar.

CHOCOLATE ÉCLAIRS:

INGREDIENTS:

For the pastry:
- 1/2 cup water
- 1/4 cup unsalted butter
- 1/2 cup all-purpose flour
- Pinch of salt
- 2 large eggs

For the filling:
- 1 1/2 cups heavy cream
- 1/4 cup powdered sugar
- 1 teaspoon vanilla extract

For the chocolate glaze:
- 4 ounces dark chocolate, chopped
- 1/2 cup heavy cream

INSTRUCTIONS:

1. Turn the oven on and set it to 400°F (200°C). Put parchment paper on a baking sheet.
2. In a pot, mix the water and butter together. Melt the butter and bring the whole thing to a boil over medium heat.
3. Turn down the heat and add the flour and salt at the same time. Stir the mixture quickly and hard with a wooden spoon until it forms a ball and pulls away from the pan's walls.
4. Take the pan off the burner and let the liquid cool for a few minutes.
5. In a different bowl, beat the eggs. Add the beaten eggs to the dough one at a time, beating well after each one until the dough is smooth and shiny.
6. Put the dough in a sewing bag with a round plain tip.
7. Spread the dough in 4–5-inch-long strips on the prepared baking sheet, leaving room between each éclair.
8. Bake the éclairs in an oven that has been warm for 20 to 25 minutes or until they are puffed and golden brown. Turn off the oven and let them cool for 5 minutes in the oven with the door cracked open a bit.

9. Remove the éclairs from the oven and set them on a wire rack to cool fully.
10. Heavy cream, powdered sugar, and vanilla extract should be mixed together in a bowl until soft peaks form.
11. When the éclairs have cooled down, cut them in half across. Fill the bottom half of each éclair with whipped cream using a spoon or a piping bag.
12. Put the chopped dark chocolate in a heat-safe bowl to make the chocolate glaze. Heat the heavy cream in a pot until it starts to bubble. Pour the hot cream over the chopped chocolate and let it sit for a minute so the chocolate can melt. Mix the ingredients until they are smooth and well blended.
13. Dip the top half of each éclair into the chocolate glaze and put it back on top of the filled bottom half.
14. Wait until the chocolate sauce is set to serve it.

COCONUT ROCHERS:

INGREDIENTS:
- 2 large egg whites
- 1/2 cup granulated sugar
- 1 teaspoon vanilla extract
- 2 cups unsweetened shredded coconut

INSTRUCTIONS:
1. Turn the oven on and set it to 325°F (160°C). Put parchment paper on a baking sheet.
2. Beat the egg whites in a bowl until they get foamy. Add the powdered sugar slowly while beating until the mixture gets thick and shiny. Add the vanilla extract and mix well.
3. Mix in the coconut shreds until everything is well mixed.
4. Spoon small mounds of the coconut mixture onto the baking sheet that has been prepped.
5. Bake the coconut rochers in an oven that has already been hot for about 15 to 20 minutes or until they are golden brown.

6. Remove the baking sheet from the oven and leave the coconut rochers on it to cool fully.
7. Once the coconut rochers have cooled, keep them at room temperature in a container that won't let air in.

CHOCOLATE FINANCIERS

INGREDIENTS:
- 1/2 cup unsalted butter
- 1 cup powdered sugar
- 1/2 cup almond flour
- 1/4 cup all-purpose flour
- 1/4 cup cocoa powder
- 4 large egg whites
- 1 teaspoon vanilla extract
- 1/4 teaspoon salt
- 1/2 cup chocolate chips or chopped chocolate

INSTRUCTIONS:
1. Turn the oven on and set it to 350°F (175°C). Grease a small muffin tin or a financier mold.
2. Melt the butter in a pot over medium heat until it turns golden brown and smells like nuts. Take it off the heat and let it cool down a bit.
3. Mix the powdered sugar, almond flour, all-purpose flour, and cocoa powder in a bowl with a whisk.
4. Whisk the egg whites in a different bowl until they get foamy. Add the vanilla extract and salt, and keep mixing until the mixture is frothy.
5. Pour the egg white mixture into the dry ingredients and gently fold them together until they are mixed.
6. Pour the melted butter in slowly while stirring the batter until it is smooth and well mixed.
7. Add the chocolate chips or pieces of chocolate and mix.
8. Fill the small muffin tins, or financier molds about 3/4 of the way with the batter.

9. Bake in an oven that has already been hot for about 12 to 15 minutes or until the tops of the financiers look cracked.
10. Take them out of the oven and let them cool for a few minutes in the molds before moving them to a wire rack to finish cooling.
11. Chocolate financiers should be served at room temperature. They can be kept for a few days in a container that keeps out air.

CHAPTER:13
SPECIAL OCCASION DESSERTS

BÛCHE DE NOËL (YULE LOG):

INGREDIENTS:
For the cake:
- 4 large eggs separated
- 1/2 cup granulated sugar
- 1/2 cup all-purpose flour
- 1/4 cup cocoa powder
- 1 teaspoon vanilla extract
For the filling:
- 1 1/2 cups heavy cream
- 1/4 cup powdered sugar
- 1 teaspoon vanilla extract
For the frosting:
- 1 1/2 cups heavy cream
- 1/4 cup powdered sugar
- 1/4 cup cocoa powder

INSTRUCTIONS:
1. Turn the oven on and set it to 350°F (175°C). Line a jelly roll pan with parchment paper that has been greased.

2. In a bowl, beat the egg whites and sugar until they are light and fluffy. Add the vanilla extract and mix well.
3. Mix the flour and cocoa powder in a different bowl with a whisk.
4. Beat the egg whites in another bowl until stiff peaks form.
5. Fold the dry ingredients into the egg yolk mixture slowly, and then fold the beaten egg whites in softly.
6. Spread the batter out evenly in the jelly roll pan that has been set up.
7. Bake the cake in an oven that has already been heated for about 12 to 15 minutes or until it bounces back when lightly pushed.
8. In the meantime, make the filling by mixing the heavy cream, powdered sugar, and vanilla extract until soft peaks form.
9. Take the cake out of the oven and let it sit for a few minutes so it can cool down. Place it on a clean dish towel.
10. Spread the filling of whipped cream all over the cake.
11. Starting at one end, carefully roll the cake into a log form with the towel. Put the side with the seam down.
12. Mix the heavy cream, powdered sugar, and cocoa powder together until stiff peaks form.
13. Using a spoon or piping bag, frost the rolled cake with the chocolate cream so that it looks like a log.
14. Use a fork or a knife to make designs on the frosting that look like bark.
15. Put powdered sugar, chocolate sprinkles, or meringue mushrooms on the log to make it look nice.
16. Before you serve the bûche de Nol, put it in the fridge for at least two hours.

GALETTE DES ROIS (KING'S CAKE):

INGREDIENTS:
- 2 sheets puff pastry, thawed
- 1 cup almond flour
- 1/2 cup granulated sugar
- 1/2 cup unsalted butter, softened
- 2 large eggs
- 1 teaspoon vanilla extract
- 1/4 teaspoon almond extract
- 1 dried fava bean or small figurine (optional)
- 1 egg yolk, beaten (for egg wash)
- Powdered sugar (for dusting)

INSTRUCTIONS:
1. Turn the oven on and set it to 400°F (200°C). Put parchment paper on a baking sheet.
2. Cream the almond flour, granulated sugar, melted butter, eggs, vanilla extract, and almond extract until everything is well mixed.
3. Put one sheet of puff dough on the ready baking sheet. Spoon the almond filling into the middle of the pastry, leaving a line around the edges.
4. Put the dried fava bean or small figurine somewhere in the filling, but be sure to tell your guests.
5. Brush some water along the edge of the dough. Put the second puff pastry sheet on top of the filling and press the sides together to seal.
6. Make designs on the top of the galette with a knife to make it look nice.
7. For a shiny finish, brush the top of the galette with beaten egg yolk.
8. Bake the galette in an oven that has already been warm for about 25 to 30 minutes or until golden brown and puffy.
9. Remove it from the oven and let it cool for a few minutes before dusting it with powdered sugar.

10. The galette des Rois can be served warm or at room temperature.

FRAISIER CAKE (STRAWBERRY AND CREAM CAKE):

INGREDIENTS:

For the cake:
- 2 cups cake flour
- 2 teaspoons baking powder
- 1/4 teaspoon salt
- 1/2 cup unsalted butter, softened
- 1 cup granulated sugar
- 3 large eggs
- 1 teaspoon vanilla extract
- 1/2 cup milk

For the filling:
- 2 cups fresh strawberries, sliced
- 2 cups heavy cream
- 1/4 cup powdered sugar
- 1 teaspoon vanilla extract

For the glaze:
- 1/4 cup strawberry jam
- 1 tablespoon water

INSTRUCTIONS:

1. Turn the oven on and set it to 350°F (175°C). Coat two 8-inch round cake pans with butter and flour.
2. Whisk the cake flour, baking powder, and salt together in a bowl.
3. In another bowl, beat the melted butter and granulated sugar together until they are fluffy and light.
4. The eggs should be added one at a time, and then the vanilla extract.

5. Add the dry ingredients and milk to the butter mixture in small amounts. Start with the dry ingredients and end with them.
6. Split the batter evenly between the ready cake pans.
7. Bake the cakes in an oven that has already been heated for 20 to 25 minutes, or until a toothpick put into the middle of one of the cakes comes out clean.
8. Take the cakes out of the oven and let them cool for 10 minutes in the pans. Then put them on a wire rack so they can cool totally.
9. In the meantime, make the filling by mixing the heavy cream, powdered sugar, and vanilla extract until stiff peaks form.
10. Put one cake piece on a plate to serve. On top, spread a layer of whipped cream, then a layer of sliced strawberries.
11. Put the second piece of cake on top and gently press it down.
12. In a small pot, melt and smooth out the strawberry jam and water by heating them over low heat. Take it off the heat and let it cool down a bit.
13. Brush the strawberry sauce on top of the cake, letting it drip down the sides.
14. If you want, you can decorate the top of the cake with more strawberries.
15. Before you serve the fraisier cake, put it in the fridge for at least an hour.

OPERA CAKE:

INGREDIENTS:

For the almond sponge cake:
- 1/2 cup almond flour
- 1/2 cup powdered sugar
- 2 large eggs
- 2 tablespoons all-purpose flour
- 1 tablespoon unsalted butter, melted

For the coffee syrup:
- 1/2 cup strong coffee
- 1 tablespoon granulated sugar
- 1 tablespoon coffee liqueur (optional)

For the coffee buttercream:
- 1/2 cup unsalted butter, softened
- 1 cup powdered sugar
- 1 tablespoon instant coffee granules dissolved in 1 tablespoon hot water

For the chocolate ganache:
- 4 ounces dark chocolate, chopped
- 1/2 cup heavy cream

INSTRUCTIONS:

1. Turn the oven on and set it to 350°F (175°C). Grease and line with parchment paper a square 8-inch baking pan.
2. Mix the almond flour and powdered sugar together in a bowl with a whisk.
3. In another bowl, beat the eggs until they are white and fluffy. Add the almond flour mixture and all-purpose flour gradually, folding gently until everything is well mixed.
4. Mix in the melting butter until it is fully mixed in.
5. Pour the batter into the baking dish that has been made and spread it out evenly.
6. Bake for about 10 to 12 minutes in an oven that has already been warmed or until the cake is lightly golden and bounces back when touched.

7. Take it out of the oven and let it cool for a few minutes in the pan. Then move it to a wire rack to finish cooling.
8. In the meantime, make the coffee syrup by putting the strong coffee, granulated sugar, and (if you're using it) coffee liqueur in a small pot and heating it up. Heat over medium heat until the sugar is dissolved. Take it off the heat and let it cool down.
9. To make coffee buttercream, beat melted butter, powdered sugar, and instant coffee that has been dissolved until the mixture is smooth and creamy.
10. Put the chopped dark chocolate in a heat-safe bowl to make the chocolate sauce. Heat the heavy cream in a pot until it starts to bubble. Pour the hot cream over the chopped chocolate and let it sit for a minute so the chocolate can melt. Mix the ingredients until they are smooth and well blended.
11. To put the opera cake together, cut the almond sponge cake into two squares that are the same size.
12. Put one layer of the almond sponge cake on a plate for serving. Use the coffee syrup to paint it.
13. On top of the wet cake layer, spread a layer of coffee buttercream.
14. Place the second layer of almond sponge cake on top and gently press it down. Use the coffee syrup to paint it.
15. On top of the second cake layer, add another layer of coffee frosting.
16. Pour and spread the chocolate ganache evenly over the top of the cake.
17. Put the opera cake in the fridge for at least two hours to let the flavors mix and the ganache harden.
18. Slice the cake and serve it chilled.

CROQUEMBOUCHE (PROFITEROLE TOWER):

INGREDIENTS:

For the choux pastry:
- 1/2 cup unsalted butter
- 1 cup water
- 1/4 teaspoon salt
- 1 cup all-purpose flour
- 4 large eggs

For the filling:
- 2 cups pastry cream or whipped cream

For the caramel:
- 2 cups granulated sugar
- 1/2 cup water

INSTRUCTIONS:

1. Set the oven to 425°F (220°C) and turn it on. Put parchment paper on a baking sheet.
2. In a pot, mix the butter, water, and salt together. Melt the butter and bring the whole thing to a boil over medium heat.
3. Turn down the heat and add all of the flour at once. Stir the mixture quickly and hard with a wooden spoon until it forms a ball and pulls away from the pan's walls.
4. .Take the pan off the burner and let the liquid cool for a few minutes.
5. In a different bowl, beat the eggs. Add the beaten eggs to the dough one at a time, beating well after each one until the dough is smooth and shiny.
6. Put the dough for the choux pastries into a piping bag with a plain round tip.
7. Place small mounds on the baking sheet that has been prepared, leaving room between each one.
8. Bake the profiteroles in an oven that has been warm for about 15 to 20 minutes or until they are golden brown and puffed. Turn off the oven and let them cool for 5 minutes in the oven with the door cracked open a bit.

9. Take the profiteroles out of the oven and set them on a wire rack to cool all the way down.
10. Once the profiteroles have cooled, use a piping bag with a small round tip to fill them with pastry cream or whipped cream.
11. In a pot, mix the sugar and water together to make caramel. Heat over medium-high heat, turning the pan occasionally until the sugar has dissolved. Don't stir the sugar syrup while it's cooking. Keep cooking it until it goes a deep amber color.
12. Take the caramel off the heat and carefully dip the bottom of each filled profiterole into the hot caramel. Put the caramel-covered profiteroles in the shape of a pyramid or tower on a serving plate. Use the caramel to hold them together.
13. Drizzle any leftover caramel on top of the croquembouche to decorate.
14. Before you serve the croquembouche, let the caramel harden. If you want, you can decorate it with spun sugar or other tasty things.

FRENCH WEDDING CAKE (PIÈCE MONTÉE):

INGREDIENTS:
For the choux pastry:
- 1/2 cup unsalted butter
- 1 cup water
- 1/4 teaspoon salt
- 1 cup all-purpose flour
- 4 large eggs
For the filling:
- 2 cups pastry cream or whipped cream
For the caramel:
- 2 cups granulated sugar
- 1/2 cup water
For decoration:

- Candied almonds, spun sugar, flowers, or other edible decorations

INSTRUCTIONS:

1. Follow the same steps as the Croquembouche method to make the choux pastry, and use pastry cream or whipped cream to fill the profiteroles.
2. To make caramel, cook the sugar syrup like in the Croquembouche method until it turns a deep amber color.
3. Dip the bottom of each filled profiterole into the hot caramel, and then place them on a serving platter or cake stand in a pyramid or other shape. The caramel will hold them together.
4. Continue dipping and stacking the profiteroles to make more than one layer.
5. Decorate the piece montée with candied almonds, spun sugar, flowers, or any other food decorations you like.
6. Before you serve the French wedding cake, let the caramel set. It can be a beautiful focal point at weddings and other special events.

ST. HONORÉ CAKE:

INGREDIENTS:

For the pâte brisée (shortcrust pastry):
- 1 1/4 cups all-purpose flour
- 1/2 cup unsalted butter, cold and cubed
- 1/4 cup granulated sugar
- 1/4 teaspoon salt
- 1 large egg yolk
- 2 tablespoons ice water

For the choux pastry:
- 1/2 cup unsalted butter
- 1 cup water
- 1/4 teaspoon salt
- 1 cup all-purpose flour
- 4 large eggs

For the caramel:
- 1 cup granulated sugar
- 1/4 cup water

For the whipped cream filling:
- 2 cups heavy cream
- 1/4 cup powdered sugar
- 1 teaspoon vanilla extract

For decoration:
- Whipped cream
- Caramelized sugar
- Cherries or other desired toppings

INSTRUCTIONS:

1. Turn the oven on and set it to 375°F (190°C). Grease a pie pan with a 9-inch diameter and a removable bottom.
2. Mix the flour, butter, sugar, and salt in a food processor. Pulse the ingredients until they look like small crumbs.
3. Whisk the egg yolk and ice water together in a small bowl. Add the egg mixture to the flour mixture slowly, running the food processor until the dough comes together.
4. Move the dough to a lightly floured surface and shape it into a ball. Cover with plastic wrap and put in the fridge for at least 30 minutes.
5. Roll the dough out until it fits the tart pan. Put the dough in the pan and cut off any extra.
6. Fill the dough with pie weights or dried beans and cover it with parchment paper. About 15 minutes in an oven that has already been hot.
7. Take off the parchment paper and the weights, and bake for another 10–12 minutes or until the pastry is golden brown. Take it out of the oven and let it cool down.
8. Melt the butter for the choux dough in a saucepan over medium heat. Add the salt and water, and bring the whole thing to a boil.
9. Turn down the heat and add all of the flour at once. Stir the mixture quickly and hard with a wooden spoon until it forms a ball and pulls away from the pan's walls.

10. Take the pan off the burner and let the liquid cool for a few minutes.
11. In a different bowl, beat the eggs. Add the beaten eggs to the dough one at a time, beating well after each until the dough is smooth and shiny.
12. Put the choux pastry into a pastry bag with a big round plain tip. Small puffs of dough should be piped around the edge of the tart shell once it has cooled.
13. Bake the choux dough puffs in an oven that has already been heated for about 25 to 30 minutes or until golden brown and crisp. Take them out of the oven and let them cool down.
14. In a pot, mix the sugar and water to make caramel. Heat over medium-high heat, turning the pan occasionally until the sugar has dissolved. Don't stir the sugar syrup while it's cooking. Keep cooking it until it goes a deep amber color.
15. Dip the bottom of each choux pastry puff into the hot caramel and set them upside down on a wire rack to let the caramel harden.
16. For the whipped cream filling, beat the heavy cream, powdered sugar, and vanilla extract until hard peaks form.
17. Fill the tart shell with the filling, which is whipped cream, and smooth the top.
18. Put the bits of choux pastry covered in caramel around the edge of the tart and lightly press them into the whipped cream.
19. Add more whipped cream, caramelized sugar, cherries, or any other toppings to the St. Honoré cake.
20. Put the cake in the fridge until it's time to serve. The best time to eat it is the day it's made.

CHARLOTTE RUSSE:

INGREDIENTS:
- Ladyfingers or sponge cake slices
- 2 cups heavy cream
- 1/2 cup powdered sugar
- 1 teaspoon vanilla extract
- 1 tablespoon gelatin powder
- 1/4 cup cold water
- Assorted fresh berries for decoration

INSTRUCTIONS:
1. Line the sides of a round mold or springform pan with ladyfingers or sponge cake slices, ensuring they fit together tightly.
2. Heavy cream, powdered sugar, and vanilla extract should be mixed in a bowl until soft peaks form.
3. Sprinkle the gelatin powder over the cold water in a small bowl and let it grow for 5 minutes.
4. Place the bowl of bloomed gelatin in a larger bowl of hot water and stir until the gelatin is fully dissolved and the mixture is clear.
5. Slowly pour the gelatin dissolved into the whipped cream while beating it.
6. Pour all of the whipped cream mixture into the shape that has been set up.
7. Put the Charlotte russe in the fridge for at least 4 hours or until it is firm.
8. Before serving the charlotte russe, carefully remove it from the pan and put fresh berries on top.
9. Cut into pieces and serve cold.

RASPBERRY AND ROSE MACARON CAKE:

INGREDIENTS:

For the macarons:
- 1 3/4 cups powdered sugar
- 1 cup almond flour
- 3 large egg whites
- 1/4 cup granulated sugar
- Pink food coloring (optional)

For the raspberry filling:
- 1 cup fresh raspberries
- 1/4 cup granulated sugar
- 1 teaspoon lemon juice
- 1/2 cup unsalted butter, softened

For decoration:
- Fresh raspberries
- Edible rose petals

INSTRUCTIONS:

1. Turn the oven on and set it to 300°F (150°C). Put parchment paper on two baking sheets.
2. Pulse the powdered sugar and almond flour in a food processor until well mixed and ground into a fine powder. Put the mixture through a sieve into a big bowl and set it away.
3. In another bowl, beat the egg whites until they get foamy. Add the granulated sugar slowly as you continue to beat. Mix until hard peaks start to form.
4. Mix the powdered sugar and almond flour that have been mixed with the beaten egg whites. Add a few drops of pink food coloring and mix until the color is even.
5. Put the macaron batter into a piping bag with a round tip. Place small rings about 1 inch apart on the baking sheets that have been prepared.
6. Tap the baking sheets a few times on the counter to remove any air bubbles and make the macarons a little flatter.

7. Let the piped macarons sit at room temperature for about 30 minutes to get skin. This will help the macarons get their unique feet when they are baked.
8. Bake the macarons in an oven that has already been warm for about 15–18 minutes, or until they are firm and come off the parchment paper easily. Let them cool down completely on the baking sheets.
9. Prepare the raspberry filling while the macarons cool. Mix the strawberries, sugar, and lemon juice in a small saucepan. Cook over medium heat until the raspberries break down and the sauce thickens. Take it off the heat and let it cool down.
10. Beat the melted butter in a mixing bowl until it becomes creamy. Add the raspberry mixture left to cool, and beat until it is well-mixed and smooth.
11. The raspberry filling should be put into a sewing bag with a round tip.
12. Pair up macarons about the same size, and pipe a dollop of raspberry filling onto one shell. Put it between two other shells.
13. Repeat until all the macarons are filled.
14. Put fresh raspberries, and edible rose flowers on the macaron cake to make it look nice.

LAVENDER CRÈME BRÛLÉE:

INGREDIENTS:
- 2 cups heavy cream
- 1/4 cup culinary lavender buds
- 6 large egg yolks
- 1/2 cup granulated sugar, plus extra for caramelizing

INSTRUCTIONS:
1. Turn the oven on and set it to 325°F (165°C). Six ramekins should be put in a baking dish.
2. Over medium heat, bring the heavy cream and lavender buds to a simmer in a pot. Take it off the burner and let it sit for 10 minutes.
3. Whisk the egg whites and granulated sugar together in a bowl until they are well mixed.
4. Whisk the cream that has been infused with lavender into the egg yolk mixture slowly, removing the lavender buds as you go.
5. Give each dish an equal amount of the mixture.
6. Put the baking dish with the ramekins in the oven. Carefully pour hot water into the baking dish until it comes about halfway up the walls of the ramekins.
7. Bake the crème brûlée for about 40 to 45 minutes, or until the edges are set, but the middle is still a little bit soft.
8. Take the ramekins out of the water bath and let them cool to room temperature.
9. Once the ramekins have cooled, cover them with plastic wrap and put them in the fridge for at least 2 hours or overnight to set.
10. Just before you serve the crème brûlée, sprinkle a thin, even layer of white sugar on top of each one.
11. Use a kitchen torch to caramelize the sugar until it turns golden brown and makes a crunchy crust.
12. Let the crème brûlées sit for a few minutes to set the sugar.
13. Serve the lavender crème brûlées chilled.

CHOCOLATE MARQUISE:

INGREDIENTS:
- 8 ounces dark chocolate, chopped
- 1/2 cup unsalted butter
- 4 large eggs separated
- 1/4 cup granulated sugar
- 1/4 cup strong coffee, cooled
- 1 teaspoon vanilla extract
- Pinch of salt
- Whipped cream and chocolate shavings for garnish

INSTRUCTIONS:
1. Grease a cake pan or a mold that can hold about 4 cups of food and line it with plastic wrap, leaving a little extra so it's easy to take out.
2. Put the dark chocolate and butter pieces in a bowl that can take the heat. Place the bowl over a pot of water that is simmering, but don't let the water hit the bottom of the bowl. Stir the mixture every so often until the butter and chocolate have melted, and the mixture is smooth. Take it off the heat and let it cool down a bit.
3. In a bowl, beat the egg whites and sugar until they are light and fluffy.
4. Mix the coffee, vanilla extract, and salt into the egg yolk mixture in a slow, steady stream.
5. Whisk the chocolate mixture slowly into the egg yolk mixture until everything is well mixed.
6. Beat the egg whites in a different bowl until stiff peaks form.
7. Fold the egg whites that have been beaten gently into the chocolate mixture until no white streaks are left.
8. Pour the chocolate mixture into the shape that has already been set up and smooth the top.
9. Cover with the plastic wrap that hangs over and put in the fridge for at least 4 hours or until firm.
10. To serve, use the plastic wrap to lift the chocolate marquise out of the shape.

11. Slice the marquise and put whipped cream and chocolate bits on top.

ÎLES FLOTTANTES (FLOATING ISLANDS):

INGREDIENTS:
For the meringues:
- 4 large egg whites
- 1/2 cup granulated sugar
- 1/4 teaspoon cream of tartar

For the crème anglaise:
- 2 cups whole milk
- 1/2 cup granulated sugar
- 4 large egg yolks
- 1 teaspoon vanilla extract

For the caramel sauce:
- 1/2 cup granulated sugar
- 2 tablespoons water

INSTRUCTIONS:
1. Turn the oven on and set it to 275°F (135°C). Put parchment paper on a baking sheet.
2. Beat the egg whites in a clean bowl until they get foamy. Add the cream of tartar and keep beating until the mixture forms soft peaks.
3. Gradually add the granulated sugar while beating constantly until stiff peaks form and the meringue is shiny.
4. Put six big scoops of meringue on the baking sheet that has been prepared.
5. Bake the meringues in an oven that has already been warm for 30–40 minutes or until they are dry and set. Take them out of the oven and let them cool all the way down.
6. Heat the milk in a pot until it starts to steam. Do not let it boil.
7. Whisk the granulated sugar and egg whites together in a bowl until the mixture is pale and creamy.

8. Pour the hot milk into the egg yolk mixture slowly while mixing all the time.
9. Return the mixture to the pot and cook it over medium heat, stirring constantly, until it thickens and coats the back of a spoon. Do not let it boil.
10. Take the pan off the heat and add the vanilla extract while stirring. Let the crème anglaise cool down to room temperature.
11. Mix granulated sugar and water in a different saucepan for the caramel sauce. Heat over medium heat until the sugar is dissolved.
12. Turn the heat up to high and cook the sugar syrup until it goes a deep amber color. Take it off the heat and let it cool down a bit.
13. Pour a spoonful of crème anglaise over a meringue in a serving bowl to serve.
14. Drizzle the caramel sauce over the cream anglaise and meringue. Do the same thing with the rest of the meringues and sauces.
15. The iles flottantes should be served right away. In the crème anglaise, the meringues should float.

FRENCH FRUIT TART WITH PASTRY CREAM:

INGREDIENTS:

For the tart shell:
- 1 1/2 cups all-purpose flour
- 1/2 cup unsalted butter, cold and cubed
- 1/4 cup granulated sugar
- 1/4 teaspoon salt
- 1 large egg yolk
- 2 tablespoons ice water

For the pastry cream:
- 2 cups whole milk

- 1/2 cup granulated sugar
- 4 large egg yolks
- 1/4 cup cornstarch
- 1 teaspoon vanilla extract
  For decoration:
- Assorted fresh fruits (such as berries, kiwi, peaches, etc.)
- Apricot jam (for glazing)

INSTRUCTIONS:

1. Pulse the flour, butter, sugar, and salt in a food processor until it looks like small crumbs.
2. Whisk the egg yolk and ice water together in a small bowl. Add the egg mixture to the flour mixture slowly, running the food processor until the dough comes together.
3. Move the dough to a lightly floured surface and shape it into a ball. Cover with plastic wrap and put in the fridge for at least 30 minutes.
4. Turn the oven on and set it to 375°F (190°C). Grease a pie pan with a bottom that can be taken off.
5. Roll the dough out until it fits the tart pan. Put the dough in the pan and cut off any extra.
6. Fill the tart pan with pie weights or dried beans and line it with parchment paper. About 15 minutes in an oven that has already been hot.
7. Take out the parchment paper and the weights, and bake for another 10–12 minutes or until the tart shell is golden brown. Take it out of the oven and let it cool all the way down.
8. Heat the milk in a pot until it starts to steam. Do not let it boil.
9. Whisk the sugar, egg whites, and cornstarch together in a bowl until they are well-mixed and creamy.
10. Pour the hot milk into the egg yolk mixture slowly while mixing all the time.
11. Return the mixture to the pot and cook it over medium heat, stirring constantly, until it thickens and coats the back of a spoon. Do not let it boil.

12. Take the pan off the heat and add the vanilla extract while stirring. Let the pastry cream cool to room temperature, and then put it in the fridge until it is cold and has set.
13. Once the tart shell and pastry cream have cooled, spread the pastry cream evenly in the tart shell.
14. Decorate the top of the tart with a design of different fresh fruits.
15. Put the apricot jam in a small pot and heat it over low heat until it becomes liquid. Brush the warm apricot jam on top of the fruit to make it shiny.
16. Put the French fruit tart in the fridge until it's time to serve.

CHERRY AND ALMOND CLAFOUTIS:

INGREDIENTS:
- 1 1/2 cups fresh cherries, pitted
- 1/2 cup all-purpose flour
- 1/4 cup granulated sugar
- 1/4 teaspoon salt
- 3 large eggs
- 1 cup milk
- 1 teaspoon almond extract
- Powdered sugar for dusting

INSTRUCTIONS:
1. Turn the oven on and set it to 350°F (175°C). Grease a baking dish or ramekins for each person.
2. Spread the sliced cherries out evenly in the baking dish or ramekins that have been greased.
3. Mix the flour, sugar, and salt together in a bowl with a whisk.
4. In a different bowl, beat the eggs until they get foamy. Mix well after adding the milk and almond flavor.
5. Whisk the wet ingredients into the dry ones slowly until everything is well-mixed and smooth.
6. Pour the batter on top of the cherries in the baking dish or ramekins, making sure to cover them completely.

7. Bake the clafoutis in an oven that has already been warm for about 30–35 minutes, or until the top is set and golden brown.
8. Take it out of the oven and let it sit for a few minutes to cool down.
9. Before you serve the cherry and almond clafoutis, dust it with powdered sugar.
10. Serve at room temperature or warm.

POT DE CRÈME AU CHOCOLAT:

INGREDIENTS:
- 2 cups heavy cream
- 4 ounces dark chocolate, chopped
- 1/4 cup granulated sugar
- 4 large egg yolks
- 1 teaspoon vanilla extract
- Whipped cream and chocolate shavings for garnish

INSTRUCTIONS:
1. Heat the heavy cream in a pot over medium heat until it starts to steam. Do not let it boil.
2. Put the chopped dark chocolate in a bowl that can take the heat. Pour the hot cream over the chocolate and let it sit for a minute so the chocolate can melt.
3. Mix the ingredients until they are smooth and well blended.
4. Whisk together the granulated sugar, egg whites, and vanilla extract in a separate bowl until the mixture is pale and creamy.
5. Whisk the chocolate mixture into the egg yolk mixture in small amounts until everything is well mixed.
6. Put the same amount of the mixture into each ramekin or serving glass.
7. Place the ramekins or glasses in a baking dish and fill it halfway with hot water.

8. Bake at 325°F (165°C) in an oven that has been warmed for about 25 to 30 minutes, or until the pot de crèmes are set but still a little bit jiggly in the middle.
9. Take the cups or ramekins out of the water bath and let them cool down to room temperature.
10. After the pots de crème have cooled, cover them with plastic wrap and put them in the fridge for at least 2 hours or until they are cold and set.
11. Add a dollop of whipped cream and chocolate bits to the top of the dish before serving.

TIRAMISU À LA FRANÇAISE:

INGREDIENTS:
- 1 1/2 cups strong coffee, cooled
- 2 tablespoons coffee liqueur (optional)
- 24 ladyfingers
- 4 large eggs separated
- 1/2 cup granulated sugar
- 8 ounces mascarpone cheese
- 1/2 cup heavy cream
- Cocoa powder for dusting

INSTRUCTIONS:
1. In a shallow dish, mix the cold coffee and, if you're using it, the coffee liqueur.
2. Dip each ladyfinger for a few seconds into the coffee mixture, and then put them in a single line in a rectangular serving dish.
3. In a bowl, beat the egg whites and granulated sugar together until the mixture is pale and smooth.
4. Mix the mascarpone cheese into the egg yolk mixture and beat until everything is smooth and well-mixed.
5. Beat the egg whites in a different bowl until stiff peaks form.
6. Beat the heavy cream in another bowl until soft peaks form.

7. Mix the beaten egg whites gently into the mascarpone mixture. Then, fold the whipped cream into the mixture.
8. On the layer of ladyfingers in the serving dish, spread half of the mascarpone mixture.
9. Repeat with more ladyfingers that have been dipped and the rest of the mascarpone mixture.
10. Cocoa powder should be sprinkled on top of the tiramisu.
11. Put the tiramisu in the fridge for at least 4 hours or overnight so the flavors can blend and the dessert can set.
12. Cut into pieces and serve cold.

LEMON AND RASPBERRY ENTREMET:

INGREDIENTS:

For the almond sponge cake:
- 1/2 cup almond flour
- 1/2 cup powdered sugar
- 2 large eggs
- 2 tablespoons all-purpose flour
- 1 tablespoon unsalted butter, melted

For the lemon mousse:
- 3/4 cup lemon juice
- 2 tablespoons lemon zest
- 1 cup granulated sugar
- 4 large egg yolks
- 1 1/2 cups heavy cream
- 2 1/2 teaspoons gelatin powder
- 1/4 cup cold water

For the raspberry mousse:
- 2 cups fresh raspberries
- 1/2 cup granulated sugar
- 1 1/2 cups heavy cream
- 2 teaspoons gelatin powder
- 1/4 cup cold water

For decoration:
- Fresh raspberries

- Lemon zest

INSTRUCTIONS:

1. Turn the oven on and set it to 350°F (175°C). Grease and line with parchment paper a round 8-inch cake pan.
2. Whisk the almond flour, powdered sugar, eggs, all-purpose flour, and melted butter together in a bowl until everything is well-mixed.
3. Pour the cake batter into the pan and spread it out evenly.
4. Bake for about 12 to 15 minutes in an oven that has already been warmed or until the cake is lightly golden and bounces back when touched.
5. Take it out of the oven and let it cool for a few minutes in the pan. Then move it to a wire rack to finish cooling.
6. Mix the lemon juice, zest, sugar, and egg whites in a saucepan for the lemon mousse. Stir the mixture constantly while cooking it over medium heat until it gets thick enough to coat the back of a spoon. Take it off the heat and let it reach room temperature.
7. Sprinkle the gelatin powder over the cold water in a small bowl and let it grow for 5 minutes.
8. Place the bowl of bloomed gelatin in a larger bowl of hot water and stir until the gelatin is fully dissolved and the mixture is clear.
9. Mix the heavy cream until it forms soft peaks. Fold the lemon mixture into the whipped cream slowly until everything is well-mixed. Then, add the gelatin that has been dissolved.
10. Pour the lemon mousse over the almond sponge cake that has been left to cool in the cake pan. Smooth the top and put it in the fridge for about 2–3 hours until it's set.
11. Put fresh raspberries and granulated sugar in a pot to make raspberry mousse. Cook over medium heat, stirring every so often, until the raspberries break down and the sauce thickens. Take it off the heat and let it reach room temperature.
12. Sprinkle the gelatin powder over the cold water in a small bowl and let it grow for 5 minutes.

13. Place the bowl of bloomed gelatin in a larger bowl of hot water and stir until the gelatin is fully dissolved and the mixture is clear.
14. Mix the heavy cream until it forms soft peaks. Fold the raspberry mixture into the whipped cream slowly until everything is well-mixed. Then, add the gelatin that has been dissolved.
15. Pour the raspberry mousse on top of the lemon mousse that is already set in the pan. Smooth the top and put it in the fridge for 4-6 hours or overnight until it's completely set.
16. To serve the entremet, carefully take it out of the cake pan and put it on a serving plate.
17. Add fresh raspberries and lemon zest to the lemon and raspberry entremet to make it look nice.
18. Cut into pieces and serve cold.

CHOCOLATE MOUSSE TOWER:

INGREDIENTS:
For the chocolate mousse:
- 8 ounces dark chocolate, chopped
- 4 large eggs separated
- 1/4 cup granulated sugar
- 1 cup heavy cream
For decoration:
- Chocolate shavings
- Fresh berries
- Mint leaves

INSTRUCTIONS:
1. Melt the chopped dark chocolate in a bowl that can handle heat set over a pot of boiling water. Stir until smooth, then take it off the heat. Let it cool down a bit.
2. In a bowl, beat the egg whites and granulated sugar together until the mixture is pale and smooth.

3. Pour the melting chocolate in small amounts into the egg yolk mixture while whisking all the time.
4. Beat the egg whites in a different bowl until stiff peaks form.
5. Whip the heavy cream in another bowl until soft peaks form.
6. After beating the egg whites, gently fold them into the chocolate mixture. Then, fold the whipped cream into the mixture.
7. Pour the chocolate mousse into cups for each person or a big serving dish.
8. Put the mousse in the fridge for at least 4 hours or until it has set.
9. Add chocolate shavings, fresh fruit, and mint leaves to the top of the mousse before serving it.
10. Cool and serve.

RED BERRY SAVARIN:

INGREDIENTS:

For the savarin dough:
- 2 cups all-purpose flour
- 1/4 cup granulated sugar
- 1 packet (2 1/4 teaspoons) active dry yeast
- 1/2 teaspoon salt
- 3/4 cup warm milk
- 3 large eggs
- 1/2 cup unsalted butter, softened

For the syrup:
- 1 cup water
- 1 cup granulated sugar
- 1/4 cup rum or fruit liqueur

For the red berry topping:
- Assorted fresh berries (strawberries, raspberries, blueberries, etc.)
- Powdered sugar for dusting

INSTRUCTIONS:

1. Mix the flour, granulated sugar, yeast, and salt together in a bowl.
2. Whisk the warm milk and eggs together in a separate bowl.
3. Mix the milk and egg mixture slowly into the dry ingredients until everything is well mixed.
4. Add the butter that has been warmed and work the dough until it is smooth and elastic.
5. Let the dough rise in a warm place for about an hour or until it has doubled in size. Cover the bowl with a clean kitchen towel.
6. Turn the oven on and set it to 350°F (175°C). Grease a bundt pan or savarin shape.
7. Punch down the dough that has risen, and then put it in the greased pan and spread it out evenly.
8. Bake the savarin in an oven that has been warm for about 25 to 30 minutes or until it is golden brown and cooked all the way through. Take it out of the oven and let it cool down a bit.
9. In the meantime, make the syrup by putting the water and sugar in a pot and heating it up. Bring to a boil and cook for a few minutes or until the sugar has dissolved. Take it off the heat and add the rum or fruit liquor while stirring.
10. Pour the sauce over the savarin while it is still warm so that it can soak into the cake.
11. Let the savarin cool down all the way in the mold before taking it out.
12. Put the savarin on a serving dish and top it with fresh berries to serve. Dust with sugar powder.
13. Cut the red berry savarin into pieces and serve it at room temperature.

MERINGUE FRUIT BASKET:

INGREDIENTS:
For the meringue:
- 4 large egg whites
- 1 cup granulated sugar
- 1/2 teaspoon cream of tartar

For the filling:
- Assorted fresh fruits (such as berries, kiwi, peaches, etc.)
- Whipped cream or pastry cream

INSTRUCTIONS:
1. Put the oven to 200°F (95°C) to heat it up. Put parchment paper on a baking sheet.
2. Beat the egg whites in a clean bowl until they get foamy. Add the cream of tartar and keep beating until the mixture forms soft peaks.
3. Gradually add the granulated sugar while beating constantly until stiff peaks form and the meringue is shiny.
4. Spoon the meringue onto the baking sheet that has been prepared and shape it into a circle with raised sides so it looks like a basket.
5. Bake the meringue in an oven that has already been warm for about 1 1/2 to 2 hours or until it is dry and crisp. Turn off the oven and leave it in there until it is completely cool.
6. Once the meringue basket has cooled, carefully lift it off the parchment paper.
7. Fill the meringue basket with whipped cream or pastry cream and top it with a variety of fresh vegetables.
8. The meringue fruit basket should be served right away.

CONCLUSION

Congratulations! You have reached the end of your trip through the French Dessert Cookbook. You have already entered the magical world of French treats and learned about the art, tastes, and skills that make them special. As you put this book away, let's think about what you've learned, how you've grown as a cook, and the endless ways you can make French desserts.

We tried to capture the spirit of French dessert culture in this book by putting together a collection of timeless classics, regional favorites, and new recipes. From tiny cakes to rich candies, each recipe has been carefully and precisely made to ensure that your desserts are delicious and show the beauty and grace that define French patisserie.

Using the tips and methods in this guide gives you the confidence to try new things in the kitchen. You now know how to make crispy pie dough, temper chocolate, and whip cream to perfection. You can now add the smell of vanilla, the taste of butter, and the charm of foreign flavors to your sweets.

But this guide has shown you more than just the recipes. It has shown you French sweets' rich history, customs, and cultural importance. You've been to the busy patisseries in Paris, the cute boulangeries in the countryside, and tried the different dishes from different parts of France. Through this investigation, you now better understand the skill, creativity, and hard work that go into making each delicious treat.

As you move beyond the pages of this book, we hope you'll keep learning about French desserts. Learn all about the stories, tastes, and skills that make French sweets special. Visit shops in your area, look for new recipes and try out your versions. Personalize each treat to your taste and preferences and let your imagination run wild.

Remember that French treats are fun not just because of how they turn out but also because of how they are made. Enjoy choosing the best ingredients, whisking, folding, shaping, and waiting for the first bite. Share these treats with people you care about, and let the magic of sweets bring you joy and closeness.

Lastly, thank you from the bottom of our hearts for picking this French Dessert Cookbook. We hope it has given you ideas, given you new skills and information, and given you a love for the art of making French desserts that will last a lifetime. May every recipe you try give your life a touch of French beauty and sweetness.

So, go out into the world of French treats and make your own, try new things, and enjoy them. May your works be full of love, joy, and the obvious charm of French pastry.

Bon appétit et bonne dégustation!

Made in United States
Cleveland, OH
20 May 2025

17045176R00111